Tim Hwang

Subprime Attention Crisis

Tim Hwang is a writer, lawyer, and technology policy researcher based in New York. Previously, he was at Google, where he was the company's global public policy lead on artificial intelligence. Dubbed "the busiest man on the internet" by *Forbes*, Hwang focuses on the future of the attention economy and the geopolitics of computational power.

Subprime Attention Crisis

FSG Originals × *Logic*

FARRAR, STRAUS AND GIROUX

New York

Subprime Attention Crisis

■ ■ ■

Advertising and the Time Bomb
at the Heart of the Internet

■

Tim Hwang

FSG Originals × *Logic*
Farrar, Straus and Giroux
120 Broadway, New York 10271

Library of Congress Cataloging-in-Publication Data
Names: Hwang, Tim, author.
Title: Subprime attention crisis : advertising and the time bomb at
   the heart of the Internet / Tim Hwang.
Description: First edition. | New York : FSG Originals, Farrar, Straus and
   Giroux, 2020 | Series: FSG Originals × *Logic*
Identifiers: LCCN 2020013395 | ISBN 9780374538651 (paperback)
Subjects: LCSH: Internet advertising. | Internet marketing. | Internet
   industry. | Internet—Economic aspects.
Classification: LCC HF6146.I58 H93 2020 | DDC 659.14/4—dc23
LC record available at https://lccn.loc.gov/2020013395

Our books may be purchased in bulk for promotional,
educational, or business use. Please contact your local bookseller
or the Macmillan Corporate and Premium Sales Department at
1-800-221-7945, extension 5442, or by e-mail at
MacmillanSpecialMarkets@macmillan.com.

www.fsgoriginals.com • www.fsgbooks.com • www.logicmag.io
Follow us on Twitter, Facebook, and Instagram at @fsgoriginals
and @logic_magazine

10 9 8 7 6 5 4 3 2

Contents

■ ■ ■

Subprime Attention Crisis

Prologue

It's the first day of Programmatic I/O, which bills itself as "the world's largest semi-annual gathering of the data-driven marketing ecosystem." Attendees pack into the basement of the San Francisco Marriott Marquis to hear talks about the finer points of online advertising. Sessions promise to explore topics like "best practices for advanced TV measurement" and "the future of video ad serving." Vendor booths fill the event, hawking everything from marketplaces for the buying and selling of ad-targeting data to elaborate platforms for automating the creation of ad content. My complimentary tote bag will fill with brochures promising "data monetization with bulletproof tech" and products that make "ideation, production and approvals of your branded content . . . streamlined with unprecedented efficiency."

This is the dark beating heart of the internet. Digital advertising—the highly automated, data-driven ecosystem represented by conferences like Programmatic I/O—is the money machine that has fueled the meteoric rise of the most prominent tech giants and content creators of the modern era. In 2020 the business of the internet is, by and large, an advertising business. Advertising in digital media generated an estimated $273.3 billion in global revenue in 2018.[1] And this amount is poised to increase: industry analysts estimate that the online advertising market will grow to $427.3 billion by the year 2022.[2]

This dazzling growth makes one of the opening talks of the day all the more puzzling. I'm sitting in the front row at a speech being given by Nico Neumann, an affable assistant professor at the Centre for Business Analytics at Melbourne Business School. His talk is titled "How Wrong Audience Targeting and AI-Driven Campaigns Undermine Brand Growth."

Nico is distinctly unlike the other speakers who fill the schedule for the rest of the day. For one, he's an academic researcher, not a marketer or a representative from a company selling products to marketers. For another, he seems intent on dismantling the entire premise of the conference in the twenty minutes allotted to his talk.

Nico focuses on a central assumption of Programmatic I/O: that algorithmically targeted advertising enhanced with scads of data about consumers *works*. Not only that it works, but that it is markedly better than the old "spray and pray" approach, where advertisers would make intuitive, seat-of-the-pants judgments about what messages would work best with consumers. This belief is sacrosanct among digital advertisers: at the most fundamental level, it is necessary to accept that a data-driven approach to creating and distributing ads works in order to justify the colossal amounts of funding that go into it.

Nico begins by showing an analysis done by him and

his collaborators auditing a sample of the third-party con-sumer data—also known as a record of everything you and I supposedly do online—that form the basis of online ad targeting. When compared with verified data about those same consumers, the accuracy was often extremely poor. The most accurate data sets still featured inaccura-cies about 10 percent of consumers, with the worst having nearly 85 percent of the data about consumers wrong.[3]

This gets worse. Targeted advertising is significantly more expensive than nontargeted advertising. Nico shows evidence that—even in the best possible case—the cost of these ads may make their overall return negative be-cause they rely on a foundation of shoddy and inaccurate data that fail to have any significant influence on sales.

Nico moves on to talk about the algorithms that are used in targeting and optimizing ads. Like many indus-tries, advertising has been caught up in the hype around artificial intelligence and machine learning because these technologies hold out the promise of targeting customers even better than before. But the technologies are correla-tion machines, says Nico; they blindly attribute success to online ads without accounting for the fact that in many cases the people advertised to would have bought the prod-uct or service anyway. One experiment he presents shows that, under proper experimental conditions, the impact of an ad for auto insurance actually had a negative effect on sales, rather than the massively positive one suggested by popular statistical models used in the industry.

So why does Nico think these technologies are so pop-ular in the online advertising space? Marketers, he says, "love machine-learning/AI campaigns because they always look so great in . . . analytics dashboards and attribution models." This cutting-edge technology is favored—in other words—because it makes for great theater.

Nico is being very friendly and polite about all this as he goes on. But the core of his talk remains: the data used in targeting ads are garbage. The algorithms being used to deliver advertising are garbage. Nico concludes that old-school mass marketing, without targeting and audience data, will "create better ROIs in many situations."[4] The whole edifice of online advertising is, in short, bunk.

This was a wild way to kick off a conference like Programmatic I/O, which is grounded in the notion that data and algorithms work and that technology is revolutionizing advertising. I start looking around to try to gauge audience reactions, expecting to see headshakes of disapproval or at least some skeptical eyebrows. Nothing. The session wraps up, and Nico asks if there are any questions. In a conference hall of hundreds of marketers, not one hand goes up.

An awkward silence pervades for a beat. Nico is led off the stage by a conference staffer and is soon replaced by a speaker excitedly explaining the benefits of advertising on Instagram. Back to your regularly scheduled programming.

It was a stark transition. Throughout the day, I kept thinking about Nico's talk. How could an industry so steadfastly ignore such significant problems in the plumbing of online advertising? Was this mere indifference, a lack of understanding, or a sign of something deeper and more pervasive within the industry? What are the implications for the rest of the internet, which depends so much on functioning advertising infrastructure to continue its past few decades of explosive growth?

Understanding these structural weaknesses requires a dive deep into the financial underpinnings of the web, a journey into the vast global plumbing that we infrequently think about but that is at the very core of why the internet is the way it is. What we discover, when we get there, is less a picture of modern, data-driven wizards of consumer persuasion, and more a murky story of perverse incentives, outright fraud, and a web economy on the brink.

Introduction

Though we frequently forget about it nowadays, the idea that the internet would give rise to some of the largest and most profitable businesses in the world was not at all obvious at the outset. In 1996, Viacom's CEO, Ed Horowitz, was able to remark dismissively that "the Internet has yet to fulfill its promise of commercial success. Why? Because there is no business model."[1]

The answer to the question of how to make boatloads of money on the internet has been, resoundingly, advertising. From the biggest technology giants to the smallest startups, advertising remains the critical economic engine underwriting many of the core services that we depend on every day. In 2017, advertising constituted 87 percent of Google's total revenue and 98 percent of Facebook's total revenue. Advertising funds the production of online content. From long-standing publications like *The New York Times* to more recent outlets like *BuzzFeed*, advertising remains the core business model for online media despite massive technological changes over the decades.

Digital advertising is highly consolidated. It is dominated by a few major types of advertising and a few major companies. Search advertising, in which ads are placed alongside search engine results, accounts for about 46 percent of overall digital ad revenue.[2] Google, not surprisingly, dominates this segment, accounting for 78 percent of the overall revenue from online searches.[3] Display advertising—where the ads are delivered through image "banners" or similar media on a website—accounts for another 32 percent of overall digital ad revenue.[4] Facebook is the biggest player in this segment, capturing about 39 percent of ad dollars spent in this format.[5] Advertising delivered through formats other than search and display (such as video, audio, or other media) makes up a far smaller part of the revenue pie.[6] Google controls around 37.2 percent of the overall U.S. digital ad spend, accounting for around $40 billion.[7] Facebook controls another $21 billion of this market, accounting for another 19.6 percent of the U.S. market.[8]

This path for funding the web has had major implications on the development of the technology itself. Core services like online search and social media are available free of charge in large part because advertisers underwrite the costs of developing them. The basic building blocks of our present-day experience of the web—from the "user profile" to the "like"—allow advertisers to more effectively target messages to users.

While advertising has made services online more accessible, numerous voices have long pointed out that advertising has generated its own fair share of negative impacts as well. In *The Attention Merchants*, the law professor Tim Wu argues that the ever-expanding reach of advertising is responsible for the "widespread sense of attentional crisis" produced by the modern technological environment.[9] The researcher Zeynep Tufekci has noted that the "deep surveillance-based profiling" and "bias toward inflammatory content" that are endemic online are natural outcomes of an advertising-based business model.[10] Investigations into Russian meddling in the 2016 U.S. presidential election have underscored the degree to which advertising channels can be leveraged to enable state-sponsored campaigns of propaganda and disinformation.[11]

These concerns are even shared by the creators of the services that have come to dominate the web. Infamously, Google's cofounders, Larry Page and Sergey Brin, worried about the perverse incentives of advertising in their seminal 1998 paper laying out the rudiments of the core algorithm behind web search. "The goals of the advertising business model do not always correspond to providing quality search to users," they wrote. "We expect that advertising funded search engines will be inherently biased towards the advertisers and away from the needs of the consumers."[12]

In the midst of all this criticism, it's worth taking a moment to think about what precisely advertising is. Media buyers—whether they are a global company, a mom-and-pop shop, or a nefarious band of trolls seeking to influence an election—are all looking to get their message in front of people. Online platforms—whether they are a billion-user social media platform or a small neighborhood newsletter—offer ways to get that message to those people. The platforms sell access to their users, and the buyers pay to acquire that access to distribute their message.

Buyers and sellers. At its core, advertising is a *marketplace* for attention. When your eyes breeze over an advertisement as you scroll through your news feeds or read an article, a transaction has occurred. Your attention has been sold by the platform and bought by the advertiser.

Even though all markets involve some kind of buying and selling, not all markets are made equal. The kinds of buying and selling that take place in a rural farmers market, for instance, are vastly different from what takes place every day on the New York Stock Exchange. We can distinguish between different types of markets in lots of different ways. Are people trading for their own livelihoods, or are they speculators looking for opportunities for profit? Are there a lot of buyers and a small number of sellers in the market? The opposite? What is being sold? How much of it is there? How easy is it to close a transaction?

Markets come in many shapes and sizes. They also are entwined with society in different ways. Changes in the marketplace for oil have wide-ranging impacts that can shape the entire course of the global economy. The failure of a local coffee shop may cause an appreciable impact only on the surrounding neighborhood. In other words, it is not enough just to think of the internet as an attention marketplace. To fully understand the implications for society at large, we must ask precisely what kind of marketplace online advertising is.

This book explores exactly this question. Advertising as a marketplace for attention has undergone major structural changes in the past decades, largely driven by the rise of the internet. As a result, the practice of buying and selling billboards in the *Mad Men* era of the 1960s bears little resemblance to the modern-day marketplace of online advertising.

Today, online advertising is more Wall Street than local bookfair. The exchange of attention is facilitated through a massive global system of digital marketplaces. Attention is not just for sale online: it has been automated and streamlined in ways that we often fail to appreciate.

As they do in modern-day capital markets, machines dominate the modern-day ecosystem of advertising on the web. This method, known in the industry as *programmatic* advertising, leverages software to automate the buying and selling of advertising inventory.

This is how Facebook and Google—the dominant duopoly—sell the attention they capture on their platforms. But, even beyond these leading companies, advertising both online and offline is increasingly bought and sold by machines. Search advertising, which was the first form to fully adopt this approach, is almost entirely transacted in a programmatic way. Programmatic advertising is dominating the other segments of the digital advertising market as well. As of 2017, programmatic advertising claimed fully 78 percent of the total digital display ad spending in the United States, representing more than $32 billion of activity.[13] This trend is set to grow, with projections showing this amount to increase to 86 percent in 2021 as automation continues to replace human buyers and sellers in this marketplace.[14]

New channels of advertising have also become integrated into the programmatic ecosystem. Advertising distributed alongside online video is now mostly facilitated through this method, accounting for 76.5 percent of the total U.S. digital video ad spend.[15] It accounted for some 74.1 percent of U.S. ad spending on mobile advertising in 2017.[16] The share of dollars going into programmatic advertising in each of these domains is also projected to rise in the coming years.[17] The global infrastructure of programmatic advertising makes it possible to access a seemingly limitless well of opportunities to place ads.

These markets have also radically expanded the scope of who can participate. Programmatic advertising tools are increasingly streamlined for easy use by nonexperts, enabling everyone from the marketing department of Coca-Cola to a local hobbyist blogger to buy and sell attention online. Sophisticated tools for targeting ads and analyzing audiences are more and more available, giving even private individuals the ability to deliver advertisements with a precision that would have been considered unthinkable to the biggest multinationals just a few decades ago.

This was not a foregone conclusion. In an alternative universe, advertising might still have ended up the dominant business model for the web, but the marketplace might have been structured in a very different way depending on how certain choices were made in the history of its development. Markets are designed and implemented by people. Those people make decisions around these economies that subsequently have wide-ranging impact.

In this respect, the resemblance of the online advertising marketplace to the financial markets is no accident. This book investigates the fascinating connections between the finance industry and the evolution of the modern programmatic advertising ecosystem. Financial markets have served as a major source of inspiration in the design of the online ad economy throughout its history, and many of the founding leaders who built these marketplaces hailed from previous careers as brokers and traders in finance.

Why does this matter? Telling this history and exploring these nuances are more than just academic exercises. Because advertising is responsible for such a colossal portion of the money that drives the internet, it is impossible to think about the future of the web without thinking about the future of advertising. Shifts in how attention is bought and sold will have major consequences not only for our everyday experience of the web but also for how the internet affects broad questions of expression, identity, and democracy.

On this count, the parallels between the financial markets and the attention markets reveal crucial hints about what the internet might be evolving toward. Indeed, the rush to architect the buying and selling of attention in the model of the financial markets raises the question of whether some of the problems of the financial markets will follow the attention economies of the web.

There is good reason to believe that the financial foundations of the web are perhaps shakier than we think, maybe even producing the conditions for a "subprime" crisis in attention, similar to the dynamics that brought down the global economy in 2008. Examining these parallels is a key step toward thinking about how society, if it's not too late, might want to re-architect the web for the better, and about whether the web as we understand it will endure.

1

The Plumbing

The jargon of programmatic advertising evokes a vision of the Wall Street of the 1980s. "Trade desks" buy and sell "inventory" on "exchanges." You might imagine something out of movies like *The Wolf of Wall Street* and *Trading Places*: big, cavernous rooms packed with shouting traders in colorful vests. But this vision of how business is done is long out-of-date. The reality resembles the ultra-quantitative, high-frequency trading of Michael Lewis's *Flash Boys* more than it does the predigital, smoke-filled rooms of *Mad Men*.

The manual processes for negotiating the sale of advertising inventory have been replaced over time with something far more mechanized. The trading floors of the global exchanges for attention are a mostly silent affair, a global network of humming servers and software that buy and sell slices of attention millions of times per second. In this marketplace, the advertiser operates as a mere supervisor to a large-scale, data-driven, automated process. This transition has been made necessary as the speed of transactions in this marketplace has outstripped the ability of any human to keep up.

A Tour of Programmatic Advertising

Being served an ad online is the textbook case of an unre-markable experience. You load up a website or an app on your phone, and an ad appears alongside, in front of, or under the thing that you wanted to see. It's a small distrac-tion as you browse around online, and for the most part it goes unnoticed. If you—like millions of others—have installed an ad blocker on your phone or web browser, you may never see these advertisements at all. It's difficult to recall clearly the last five or six ads that you might have run into online. It's probably even more difficult to recall the last time that you actually clicked on one.

Yet this boring, mundane occurrence online belies the intricate machinery running under the hood of each and every one of these ads. The modern online advertising ecosystem is a mind-bending, globe-spanning infrastruc-ture designed to deliver billions of advertisements at split-second speeds every minute of every day. What you see at the end point—a banner advertisement that you may instantly forget, or a preroll video that you click to skip as quickly as you can—is only the tiniest piece of an in-credibly complex system that is otherwise invisible as you move through the internet.

The players in the marketplace for attention are the same as they always have been: those who have attention they are willing to sell, and those who are willing to buy. In online advertising parlance, those who sell attention are the "publishers." Attention can be captured in many different ways. A YouTube star who has millions of viewers tuning in to see her latest video and a social media platform where users are logging on to chat and comment on each other's photos are examples of publishers with a surplus of attention—other people's attention—to sell. Publishers sell "inventory": the opportunity for the buyer to display its message to someone who is paying attention to the publisher. The buyers vary: they include large companies buying advertising to promote their products and marketing agencies working on their behalf, as well as what are known as agency trading desks—specialized companies focused on navigating the programmatic advertising ecosystem.

The infrastructure of programmatic advertising is architected so that, theoretically, publishers are able to sell their inventory of attention to the highest bidder among a pool of buyers. This is generally done through an arrangement known as real-time bidding (RTB). RTB is initiated by the tiniest of actions—clicking on a link or loading a piece of content—which sets off a rapid, orderly cascade of events, Rube Goldberg–style. As soon as an opportunity for delivering an advertisement appears, an ad server leaps into action, announcing to the marketplace the opportunity to bid for inventory.

One of the most incredible aspects of the RTB system is that the entire process takes place *in real time*. The advertisements you see online are not predetermined. At the moment you click the link and load up the page, a signal from the ad server triggers an instantaneous auction to determine which ad will be delivered. The highest bidder gets to load its ad on the website and into your eyeballs.

This process happens at the speed of light. The inventory must be bid upon and the actual advertisement delivered in the split-second moment between when you click to load something online and the time that the website or content on an app is finally loaded. The entire process of putting out a request for bids, making the bids, evaluating the bids, and delivering the advertisement takes place in under a hundred milliseconds—about a quarter of the time it takes you to blink.[1] This happens millions and millions of times across the internet every second, without ceasing and largely without hiccups.

This combination of rapid bidding and massive scale means that humans cannot be directly responsible for initiating the auction, bidding, and evaluating the bids. There simply is not enough time. Programmatic advertising is facilitated entirely through software platforms that automate this process. These are known as demand-side platforms (DSPs) or supply-side platforms (SSPs). DSPs service the buyers, providing tools to specify certain parameters around their bidding and specify the audiences they would like to target. SSPs provide a suite of tools that are a mirror image of this for publishers, enabling sellers to specify auction rules, set price floors, and control the kinds of advertisers able to gain access to their inventory.

Once configured manually, programmatic advertising relies on the interactions between algorithms to make the discrete choices to bid on available blobs of advertising inventory. These competing algorithms working on behalf of ad buyers then interact with algorithms working on behalf of the publisher, which choose the winner of the auction and deliver the selected advertisement.

As with the Nasdaq and the New York Stock Exchange, the buying and selling of advertising inventory does not take place all in one location. There exists a dense, networked set of ad exchanges that facilitate the meeting of supply and demand in this marketplace. At the time of this writing, companies like AppNexus, OpenX, and Smaato are leading players in this space, alongside exchanges operated by larger long-standing players like Verizon Media (formerly Oath) and Microsoft. The largest platforms—Google and Facebook—offer their advertising inventory on their own specialized tools, which operate much like a DSP for buyers.

Perhaps most remarkably, all of this takes place seamlessly. We are bombarded by ads online but give little thought to the complex, behind-the-scenes machinery of bidding and delivery that makes them possible. This invisibility belies the huge importance of this infrastructure and the implications of the failure of this system for the web and for society as a whole.

What Happens If This Breaks?

The economic significance of programmatic advertising is huge. Most obviously, the iconic services of the present-day internet—search engines, social media platforms, and more—are built on a bedrock of advertising both in the

United States and beyond. Whether it is Google or Baidu, Facebook or Weibo, all these services rely on a robust, automated market for buying and selling attention to generate revenue. But programmatic advertising is critical not just because it is the business model for a handful of dominant technology players. It is important because it is increasingly intertwined throughout the broader economy.

Certain goods and services are more interlinked throughout the economy than others. Oil is a prototypical example. The price of oil is important not only because it influences the balance sheets of the companies that extract and refine it. Its influence echoes through the economy, affecting things like the costs of transportation and of the production of certain goods. Because it forms such a fundamental part of the economies of certain nations, the price of oil shapes the balance of power among countries as well.[2]

This relative interconnectedness of particular industries has important implications for what happens to the broader economy when those industries run into trouble. One reason that the 2007–2008 subprime mortgage crisis was so damaging was that banks and other major financial institutions at the core of the economy relied on the continued health of what turned out to be shoddy mortgages. When the mortgages failed, so did the banks, which in turn were connected to a vast range of economic activities throughout the world. This served to make a downturn in the mortgage market one that placed intense pressure on other parts of the economy at the same time. Economists contrast the 2008 downturn with the 2001 dot-com bust in technology stocks, which was more isolated and had a less enduring impact in part because the tech companies were less interlinked with the rest of the economy.[3]

Programmatic advertising more closely resembles oil than an overhyped mid-1990s technology stock in this respect. For one, advertising is still the primary financial engine funding the creation of most media. The ad exchange infrastructure is deeply integrated into the online world because everyone, from independent stars on YouTube to massive media companies, leverages the programmatic advertising infrastructure. Increasingly, advertising on "nondigital" media like television, radio, and even billboards is facilitated through these global exchanges.[4]

The influence of programmatic advertising, however, extends beyond its role in bankrolling the media. The online advertising ecosystem has proven to be a highly flexible infrastructure, one that can transform products and services that weren't previously monetized through advertising into advertising businesses. It's easy to forget that products like email were originally operated as fee-based businesses in which various features like storage and spam filtering were monetized as a subscription.[5] Services like Gmail transformed this, using the advertising model to make email free to use and monetizing it through the sale of user attention.[6]

One way of looking at the interconnectedness of programmatic advertising is to follow the money, asking what kinds of businesses rely on the flow of money from these systems. It's equally revealing to follow where the wealth generated by advertising is subsequently invested.

Google is a perfect example of advertising's remarkable ability to fund other ambitious ventures. Whether underwriting a massive effort to scan the world's books or enabling the purchase of leading robotics companies, Google's revenue from programmatic advertising has, in effect, reshaped other industries.[7] Major scientific breakthroughs, like recent advances in artificial intelligence and machine learning, have largely been made possible by a handful of corporations, many of which derive the vast majority of their wealth from online programmatic advertising.[8]

Online advertising is also important for the wealth it has generated on the individual level. The advertising economy turned Mark Zuckerberg into one of the richest people in the world, and that wealth now supports a range of other endeavors. Zuckerberg has pledged Facebook shares worth more than $45 billion to his Chan Zuckerberg Initiative, which focuses on "health, education, scientific research, and energy," making it instantly one of the most well-resourced entities in these domains.[9] And for every Zuckerberg, there are thousands of other technology entrepreneurs who have made smaller, though still significant, fortunes through businesses funded by programmatic advertising. How these lucky few spend their wealth connects the fate of the advertising economy with a range of other, unrelated causes.

The fact that these invisible, silent programmatic marketplaces are critical to the continued functioning of the internet—and the solvency of so much more—begs a somewhat morbid thought experiment: What would a crisis in this elaborately designed system look like? What if the advertising revenue generated by the online attention marketplace were to decline rapidly and remain depressed for a long time?

The immediate and most obvious impact would be on the online platforms and ad exchanges themselves. There would be not just a sharp decline in the revenue generated by their core businesses but also a corresponding pinch in stock prices driven by investor panic in the financial markets. Recall that—for all their market dominance—platforms like Google and Facebook are heavily dependent on their continued revenue from advertising.

Interestingly, the impact might not immediately be felt by the everyday user of the web. Companies like Facebook and Google hold substantial reserves in cash, and they might be able to weather the short-term impact by drawing on these resources to maintain the status quo. The platforms could continue to offer their services for free to consumers in the hopes that confidence would be restored and ad buyers would return to the market. They could continue to fund product development, hire top engineers, and ensure the flow of quality snacks to their corporate campuses.

This crisis would generate an intense phase of consolidation beyond the rarefied confines of the Google-Facebook duopoly. Companies without similarly massive cash reserves would face pressure to close or merge to remain in operation. But the net effect in the short term would be that while businesses would be hurting, end users would still interact with their products and services in largely the same way.

This would be a temporary state of affairs: longer-term, the impact of this crisis would become more apparent to the average user. Intense dysfunction in the online advertising markets would threaten to create a structural breakdown of the classic bargain at the core of the information economy: services can be provided for free online to consumers, insofar as they are subsidized by the revenue generated from advertising. Companies would be forced to shift their business models in the face of a large and growing revenue gap, necessitating the rollout of models that require the consumer to pay directly for services. Paywalls, paid tiers of content, and subscription models would become more commonplace. Within the various properties owned by the dominant online platforms, services subsidized by advertising that are otherwise unprofitable might be shut down.

Imagine waking up to the announcement that searching the web would now require a monthly subscription fee, or that your favorite social network would have limited features until you added a credit card to sign up for a premium version. Imagine being charged on a per-trip basis for navigating with Google Maps. Think of WhatsApp—which was acquired by Facebook in 2014 but has not made significant money for the platform[10]—being shut down in order to preserve Facebook's bottom line. How much would you be willing to pay for these services? What would you shell out for, and what would you leave behind? The ripple effects of a crisis in online advertising would fundamentally change how we consume and navigate the web.

Silicon Valley would not be the only region hurt by such a crisis. The failure of the programmatic advertising economy would have follow-up impacts throughout the media, considering how many media businesses rely on the programmatic ecosystem. Already in 2013, a survey of publishers revealed that 72 percent of them were offering space to advertisers through automated real-time auctions.[11] Condé Nast—the leading mass media company, which owns publications like *Wired*, *The New Yorker*, *Vanity Fair*, and *GQ*—makes advertising on all of its digital properties buyable through programmatic marketplaces.[12] Because programmatic advertising is increasingly a means of selling advertising through channels other than just banner ads on websites, a downturn in this economy might negatively affect some services that you might not immediately suspect. The audio streaming service Spotify, for instance, receives 20 percent of its advertising buys through programmatic means.[13]

All of these businesses rely on the continued strength of automated advertising marketplaces to generate revenue. The obvious outcome of a downturn would be for these businesses to cut costs. We might expect a massive round of layoffs in digital media, similar to but much larger than the 2019 firings at prominent content channels like *Vice*, *BuzzFeed*, *Vox*, and *Mashable*.[14] Even a short-term decline in advertising could create massive disruptions. As the 2020 newsroom layoffs triggered by the COVID-19 outbreak show, most media businesses are not well positioned to weather even brief periods of weakness in the market for ads. Media companies dependent on online advertising might also become attractive acquisition targets for the well-resourced online platforms and other buyers in such a financially distressed environment.

Consider for a moment all of the advertising-supported media that you consume for free on a daily basis: podcasts, videos, articles, email newsletters, and more. How would it feel to have a large portion of that media suddenly disappear behind a paywall—or disappear entirely? How would your experience of the web change? What would it feel like for Facebook to announce that it was purchasing *The New York Times* or for YouTube to announce that it was purchasing *Vice*? What we consume and who controls what we consume would radically change in such an environment.

We might be able to stomach these changes as users of the web, but it's important not to lose sight of the significant human costs of such changes. Paywalls rising throughout the web would exclude large populations of consumers unable to afford services that until recently were free. A failure of the online advertising markets would have a serious impact on a wide range of journalists, videographers, and other media creators great and small. Social media and platforms like YouTube serve as free distribution channels, allowing creators to reach much broader audiences than they otherwise would. A changing business model that prioritized subscription and paid access would narrow these prospects and make content creation less sustainable. Not to mention the knock-on effects that might emerge from a radical slowing of the spigot of philanthropic funding—from supporting medical research to fighting climate change—driven by a contraction of wealth in the technology sector.

In the most dramatic case, a sustained depression in the global programmatic advertising marketplace would pose some thorny questions not entirely unlike those faced by the government during the darkest days of the 2008 financial crisis. Are advertising-reliant services like social media platforms, search engines, and video streaming so important to the regular functioning of society and the economy that they need to be supported lest they take down other parts of the economy with them? Are they, in some sense, "too big to fail"? In an era when the relationship between the government and these platforms is becoming increasingly adversarial, state action to bail out a fragile tech industry might massively reshape the relationship between the state and the internet.[15] What if the White House were to offer to keep key internet platforms solvent on the condition that they accept greater regulation and deeper involvement by government appointees in their operations?

This is a long way of saying that the web that we

experience when we roll out of our beds and unlock our phones is sustainable only because of the continued health of programmatic advertising. Change that, and the whole edifice of the economy built on top of it begins to change with it. Persistent lack of confidence in the online advertising markets would produce a web that would be more fragmented, less accessible, and stuck at a slower rate of growth quite distinct from the last few decades of rapid growth in the technology sector. Reasonable minds can disagree about whether these changes are long overdue or desirable, but it is certain that a sudden transition would be painful.

The skeptic might point out here that it is easy to imagine a doomsday scenario but quite a different thing for that speculation to become reality. Would a sustained, global collapse in programmatic advertising actually be possible? How might it come about?

Even as the world grapples with a global recession in the wake of the COVID-19 pandemic, programmatic advertising appears poised to grow, grow, grow over the long term. The dominant, ad-driven platforms of the web continue to be some of the largest and most profitable businesses in the world. Traditional forms of advertising—the dollars that put ads in newspapers and magazines, for instance—are not yet fully integrated into the ecosystem of online programmatic advertising. This means that there is room for growth: these dollars may yet become part of the ad exchange system.

But such a rosy situation may mask deeper systemic risks lurking within the system. Like the financial markets prior to the crisis of 2008, the modern infrastructure of the ad economy might have produced explosive growth while simultaneously introducing a set of vulnerabilities that could make this money machine less stable over time. Indeed, the parallels between the financial industry and the evolving economy of online advertising give us clues as to where things might be going and the less evident cracks that might lie beneath the surface.

2

Market Convergence

It is easy to take the presence of advertising on the internet as a given. The infrastructure of programmatic advertising has so robustly supported the rise of the modern giants of the technology sector and operates so efficiently that it often seems as if the internet was always meant to work this way.

That the internet was predestined to be one way or another is an attractive but ultimately wrong idea. There is nothing essential about the internet as we know it. The internet is not inherently open or democratizing, nor is it inherently closed or authoritarian. Digging into the history of the internet quickly reveals that the present-day internet is just one of many different information networks that could have come to be.[1]

In that sense, the internet has been actively designed at each stage in its history. An ever-compounding set of choices has resulted in the particular experience that we have of it today. This is true of the selection of advertising as a primary money machine for funding the web. It is also true of the precise way that we set these advertising marketplaces up.

To that end, we need to say *why* the programmatic

advertising ecosystem has ended up bearing such a close resemblance to the structure of the financial markets. What forces encouraged the online programmatic advertising marketplace to take the shape that it did? How much was coincidence, and how much was an active effort to structure the market for attention online in this precise way? How much does the rise of programmatic advertising owe to the structural similarities with finance?

This chapter argues that the resemblances between the programmatic advertising markets and the financial markets are more than skin-deep. While software engineers might have laid down the code that enabled advertising to explode as the primary moneymaker for the web, its design has been inspired not by the culture of nerds in garages but instead by the more buttoned-up world of the capital markets.

From Wall Street to Silicon Valley

Online advertising predates the rise of the internet as we know it today. Companies like America Online (AOL), Prodigy, and CompuServe were precursors to the modern web in the 1980s and 1990s, allowing customers to use their computers to access a limited "walled garden" of chat rooms, media, and shopping over their phone lines.

These services received monthly fees paid by their subscribers, but they also relied on advertising as a major source of revenue. Prodigy was pitched as "a new advertising medium . . . that would assemble audiences for marketers much as niche TV channels do."[2] AOL became a major channel through which other emerging dot-com companies of the era could advertise to prospective users.[3] AOL also experimented with allowing businesses to pay to sponsor content on the platform. CBS would pay to be the exclusive provider of sports reporting, 1-800-Flowers would pay to be the official flower delivery service, and so on.[4]

But the advertising taking place on these early platforms was still a far cry from the large-scale automation and split-second bidding of modern programmatic advertising. Myer Berlow, who ran AOL's advertising operation, hailed from the advertising world of New York and had "no experience with anything computer-related."[5] In the 1990s, the early internet was increasingly commercialized, but it was still organized in ways that relied on teams of human salespeople working to sell advertising space on these platforms.

Search engines, which were made necessary by the ever-increasing sprawl of the internet and the lack of effective tools for exploring it, would alter this model entirely. During their early years in the 2000s, search engines like Google were able to acquire huge numbers of users who relied on them to find things on the web, but these search engines faced the tricky challenge of figuring out how to make such a tool pay off as a business.[6]

Advertising was by no means the most obvious way to make operating search engines a solvent business. In its early years, Google anticipated that only about 10 to 15 percent of its revenue would be derived from advertising.[7] The rest of the revenue was assumed to come from the licensing of its "search technology to other websites . . . [and] a hardware product that would allow companies to search their own operations very quickly, called 'Google Quick Search Box.'"[8] These initial projections, of course, would soon be blown away by the torrent of money generated by advertising.

Getting advertising to work on a search engine required automation. Google pulled away from the competition by creating AdWords, a product that enabled advertisers to place promoted listings alongside search engine results. AdWords combined two contemporary advances into one efficient product.

First, Google adopted advertising auctions, an idea proposed and implemented by GoTo, an early Google competitor run by the entrepreneur Bill Gross.[9] Buyers of advertising would bid against one another for the rights to show their message when a user searched for a term like "insurance," with the winner paying a penny more than the second-highest bidder (a "Vickery second-bid auction" in economics parlance).[10] This maximized the amount paid for the advertising inventory available with each search result.

Second, Google incorporated an algorithm that assessed the quality of an ad by looking at its various elements and predicting whether users were likely to click on it. This metric would then influence the value of the bids made by various advertisers, sometimes leading a bidder offering a lower price to win the auction based on the quality of the ad. This system was intended to align incentives such that advertisers would create ads that were relevant and useful to Google users.

The combination of auctions and adjustment via a quality metric was a huge success. AdWords transformed Google from a speculative venture to one of the most profitable enterprises of the last century. From then on, there was, in the words of the journalist Steven Levy, "nothing but glory in the bottom line."[11] Other products followed, built on the infrastructure developed for AdWords. Google AdSense, which allows publishers to earn money by offering space on their websites that the platform sells to advertisers, launched soon afterward and was similarly successful.

The success of AdWords and AdSense depended on a major technical feat, which the engineering-centered culture of Google was well positioned to achieve. Coordinating and resolving a colossal number of simultaneous auctions required a high capacity to deploy reliable and robust computer systems. The development of this infrastructure was led not by an MBA but by Eric Veach, a Stanford computer science graduate whose previous work involved developing the software that rendered animations at Pixar.[12] In fact, the debut of AdWords was viewed with consternation by the existing sales team at Google. The replacement of their more traditional approach with an algorithmically driven, automated auction was seen as confirmation of their long-held suspicion that Google's cofounder, Larry Page, "wanted to do away with [the sales team] entirely."[13]

Products like AdWords originated within a pro-

foundly technical culture and were made possible by software engineers. But quite a different set of experts would
take those innovations and mold them into the present-day
programmatic advertising infrastructure. Google began
enlisting economists to manage these vast marketplaces;
the new team members viewed the algorithmic exchange
for packaging and selling attention as deeply akin to the
financial markets.

Hal Varian, who joined Google in 2002 and who
would eventually play a role as the company's chief economist, became the "godfather to the advertising effort."[14]
He would oversee a project to create a "search-word advertising equivalent of the stock market" that would divide
keywords into high-cap, mid-cap, and low-cap segments
and generate its own version of the Dow Jones Industrial
Average.[15] AdWords and AdSense changed the paradigm
for distributing advertising inventory, moving it from a
world of qualitative judgment and persuasive salespeople
to one of quantitative analysis and automated algorithms.
As Steven Levy would recount in his 2011 history of Google, "Varian realized that [Google] was the embodiment of
the Silicon Valley ethic . . . Most Internet companies were
still selling ads the way Madison Avenue had always done
it. Google saw the entire exchange differently."[16]

This adoption of the financial markets as a metaphor
for the online advertising markets was not a phenomenon
limited to Google, or even to the domain of search advertising. As the early templates of programmatic advertising
pioneered at Google became more popular as a model for
buying and selling attention, many continued to draw

inspiration from the financial markets. One *Wall Street Journal* feature reporting on the nascent platforms that would evolve into modern programmatic ad exchanges remarked that these tools allowed "selling web advertising space like pork bellies."[17] *The New York Times* observed that "quants have become a force in the advertising industry, much as they became a force on Wall Street starting in the 1970s and 80s."[18] As the hype grew around these platforms, the stock exchange was a frequent point of reference in explaining the distinctiveness of open marketplaces for ads.[19]

DoubleClick, founded in 1996 by Kevin O'Connor and Dwight Merriman, was a major player in the nascent business, helping advertisers place ads across various publishers online and measuring their performance. DoubleClick survived the 2001 dot-com crash and in 2007 launched one of the first exchanges allowing publishers and advertisers to buy and sell inventory. *The New York Times* described the platform as a "Nasdaq-like exchange." DoubleClick representatives explained it as a "mix of eBay and Sabre, the airline reservations system that travel agents use. The service . . . let advertisers see information about what competitors bid for particular ads . . . [and] let publishers try to ensure that they sell their ad spots at the highest possible price."[20] DoubleClick was acquired by Google in 2007 for $3.1 billion.[21]

Other players in this primordial phase of the online advertising market would adopt similar framings, sometimes even boasting previous careers in finance. Right Media, another early ad exchange pioneer acquired by Yahoo in 2007 for $680 million, was described by *The Wall Street Journal* as a virtual markets "where buyers and sellers of Internet ads can efficiently find one another . . . not unlike the role stock exchanges play for shares."[22] The founder and CEO, Michael Walrath, had worked at the brokerage firm D. H. Blair and the hedge fund Sands Brothers Asset Management.[23] Walrath cautioned against assuming a strict similarity, but he recognized that his platform was "loosely modeled on the stock market."[24] AdECN, another early competitor in this space, explicitly adopted the stock market model in much of its marketing and product design. AdECN's cofounder, Jeff Green, described the aim of the company as "trying to be the New York Stock Exchange of advertising."[25] When the platform launched in Britain in 2008, the CEO, Bill Urschel, called it the "equivalent of the London Stock Exchange's Big Bang in 1986 . . . That allowed the elimination of the middle man, the introduction of variable trading and electronic trading."[26] Green now runs a different ad technology company, The Trade Desk, and says that his new company uses "a system much more like the Goldman Sachs of online advertising."[27]

It is significant that the stock exchange was the model adopted by entrepreneurs who were designing the platforms that became today's programmatic advertising infrastructure. This mode of thinking was "an engine, not a camera," in the sense that it acted as "an active force transforming its environment, not a camera passively recording it."[28] The rise of programmatic advertising was not just a continuation of the commercialization of the web that was underway in the 1990s but also a process that actively shaped the rules and practices of how attention would be traded online.

There are two intertwined developments that make the modern online advertising ecosystem possible. The first is a set of technological developments. It is indisputable that certain technological advances were needed to allow AdWords to enable the buying and selling of advertising at huge scale and split-second speed without human intermediaries. But this first set of developments does not tell the whole story about how the programmatic advertising system came to be. Technology enables the game to be played, but it does not dictate the rules of that game.

The second, equally important development that gave birth to the programmatic advertising marketplace was ideological: the adoption of the mental frames of finance. Capital markets like the New York Stock Exchange served as a crucial inspiration, providing a template that early advertising technology entrepreneurs drew from in setting the rules of these novel markets in search and display advertising.

Market Commodification

How do we characterize the influence of the finance industry on the development of the business model of the internet?

One simplistic approach is to think of the entrepreneurs who constructed the modern edifice of programmatic advertising as, essentially, commercializers. The nascent open internet—the child of academic and government funding—needed to become financially sustainable as a business. The efforts of companies like GoTo and AOL served to bundle user attention online and extract money from this attention through advertising. As a result, what was formerly a sphere of nonprofit and public research was transformed into a sphere of for-profit and private enterprise.

But this version of events denies the internet its historical place as a communications platform and broadcast medium, very much the successor to the telegraph, radio, and television.[29] The transformation of attention into something monetizable is, of course, not a new phenomenon. Predigital advertising was engaged in the buying and selling of attention through billboards, newspaper ads, and television spots just as modern-day advertisers pay to grab attention online. The infrastructure of online advertising did not invent the commercialization of attention.

Thinking of the internet's transition as a simple shift from noncommercial to commercial misses an important nuance. We should distinguish mere commercialization from the specific kind of commercialization wrought by the ad technology entrepreneurs of the 1990s and 2000s. Earlier generations of advertisers bought and sold attention, but never at the speed, scale, and level of granularity characteristic of today's programmatic advertising marketplaces. What is different about the present-day online advertising system is the extent to which it has enabled the bundling of a multitude of tiny moments of attention into discrete, liquid assets that can then be bought and sold frictionlessly in a global marketplace.

Attention is *commodified* to an extent that it has not been in the past. There are many different ways of making money, and the internet could have commercialized—even through advertising—without developing the extreme level of commodification that has occurred.

Commodification may seem somewhat mystical, but it represents a fairly straightforward process of evolution that appears in many marketplaces. To get an intuition for why this might be the case, consider a hypothetical market for chickens on a small island. For an economist, the dynamics of this market are simple. The chicken farmer raises chickens and then sells them to a number of local customers, from the butcher to the sandwich shop to someone who wants to keep a chicken as a pet. This system works pretty well: the farmer can travel physically from place to place hawking a small number of chickens and haggling with potential buyers. The price at which a given chicken is sold is based on the specific characteristics of that chicken and the needs of the farmer and her buyer.

This type of market arrangement works at a small scale, but it quickly becomes awkward as the marketplace grows. Now imagine that our small island is connected to the mainland by a highway that leads to a massive city. Our farmer, who previously had to meet and haggle with only a handful of potential buyers, is now confronted with a marketplace many times greater than what she had to contend with before. The farmer suddenly has a vast number of people she might be able to sell to. Those potential buyers are likely people the farmer has never met. If that big city is connected by roads, railways, and airports to parts farther afield, the potential number of buyers could be overwhelming. Personally identifying a buyer and negotiating the price for each individual sale becomes challenging to manage effectively.

Buyers run into their own problems. Buyers might never have met our hypothetical chicken farmer. They may be far away from our island and unable to get there to evaluate the quality of the chickens. Unlike the local butcher or sandwich shop or chicken fancier, whose proximity to the farmer lets them purchase chickens as needed, the new buyers may want to buy a large number of chickens at once from a single seller. The buyer may not be able to efficiently acquire that number through a piecemeal process of buying a few chickens each from a large number of different farmers.

Standardization—the first step toward commodification—allows the market to accommodate a larger number of players. Arguably, the greatest friction in this marketplace is that buyers and sellers cannot easily assess what they are buying. It is challenging to quickly determine at a distance whether a chicken is high quality or low quality, particularly where buyers and sellers are strangers and where there is low trust between the various players in the marketplace.

Say that we bring together the buyers and sellers of chickens, and they agree on common definitions about what is traded in the marketplace. Rather than selling different types of chickens in nonstandard quantities, they specify something that we'll call a Standard Chicken Lot (SCL). The SCL is a fixed unit of chickens having certain qualities: the chickens might need to be above a certain weight, to not have any diseases, and so on. They hire some inspectors to go around to places where chickens are sold to make sure that people are conforming to this standard. On their own, chickens are a heterogeneous thing. Some are tall and some are short. Some are thin and some are heavy. Some are of one breed and others are of another. The SCL ensures that the chickens traded in our market are of a commonly understood quality and quantity.

This may not sound like a whole lot, but it changes everything. Suddenly our chicken marketplace is capable of enabling large numbers of buyers and sellers to quickly transact chickens at arm's length by simply knowing how many SCLs are on offer and for how much.

Standardization does not just allow the market to expand effectively. It also produces the second step in the process of commodification—abstraction. SCLs are abstract—disconnected from the process of production and the unique identity of the producer. Because the units of chicken being bought and sold are now standardized, a prospective buyer no longer needs to know the specific characteristics of a farmer to move ahead on a transaction. SCLs are interchangeable: an SCL produced by our island chicken farmer is the same as another SCL produced in a different place.

Abstraction enables arrangements that might never

otherwise emerge in our original island chicken marketplace. This kind of abstraction facilitates speculation.
Groups with little interest in raising chickens or consum-
ing chickens might choose to engage in buying and
selling SCLs to make money from fluctuations in price.
One could buy the rights to an SCL in the marketplace
and sell the rights at some later date, without ever seeing
or moving the actual chickens. The trade in SCLs—which
are abstract assets—can take place far away from where
the chickens are hatched and where they end up.

This is more than a just-so story; the dynamics of
commodification are very real across many different kinds
of markets. Perhaps one of the most dramatic historical
examples, as documented by William Cronon in his book
Nature's Metropolis, is the emergence of large-scale grain
markets in Chicago during the middle of the nineteenth
century.[30]

Before 1850, grain was bought and sold in large, open-
air marketplaces near the waterfront of Chicago.[31] These
marketplaces transacted grain in very much the same way
as our island chicken farmer sells chickens. Grain was
sent by the sackful from a farm to a merchant, who would
haggle face-to-face with buyers in an effort to obtain the
best price. The merchant acted as a middleman for the
farmer, who retained ownership over his grain and paid
the merchant a commission for each sale.

As Cronon explains, the rise of the railroads transformed this mode of exchange and "transmute[d] wheat
and corn into monetary abstractions."[32] Railroads allowed
crops to be efficiently transported from outlying farms

into Chicago, rapidly increasing the amount of grain that entered the city's market. When it became clear that bulk grain was more efficiently sold at market, traditional grain sacks were abandoned and farmers pooled their crops into freight cars.[33] But combining grain from different farms raised the question of how to deal with the ownership of the grain that each farmer contributed to a given carload.

A private industry consortium, the Chicago Board of Trade (CBOT), eventually solved the problem through standardization. The CBOT designated three categories of grain and four levels of quality ("Club," "No. 1," "No. 2," and "Rejected").[34] Farmers putting grain into a train car received a receipt indicating a quantity of grain and a quality level. The receipt was redeemable for an equal quantity of the same quality grain—not the *same* grain, but its functional equivalent.

Once standardized, grain became abstracted into a commodity. The receipts could be bought and sold without regard to the specific identity of the farmer who originally produced the grain. People with no interest in grain production could make a profit by buying and selling receipts. Famously, the CBOT also facilitated the rise of a vigorous trade in "futures," speculative contracts betting on the future price of grain. According to Cronon, grain came to be seen "as a commodity, not as a living organism planted and harvested by farmers as a crop for people to mill into flour, bake into bread, and eat."[35]

Another outcome of grain commodification was an explosion in the size and importance of the market itself.

Chicago commodified faster than other grain markets, outstripping its longtime rival St. Louis in 1855.[36] Before commodification, grain produced in the northern United States was sold to markets in southern states. After commodification, the trade reversed direction. "No place was more important than Chicago to this redirection of agricultural trade," Cronon writes.[37] The CBOT remained the world's dominant commodities market and futures exchange well into the twentieth century.[38]

The economics of nineteenth-century grain may seem far removed from the online advertising markets of the twenty-first century. But the huge distances of time mask deep parallels. Attention—a varied, heterogeneous, hard-to-define thing—underwent a similar process of commodification over the course of the 2000s, culminating in the programmatic marketplace.

The Commodification of Attention

In many respects, "attention" is completely different from grain and chickens. After all, chickens and grain are real, tangible objects. Attention is bafflingly abstract. It exists for a moment and then drifts somewhere else. Chickens have certain clear, measurable attributes. They can be old or young, sick or healthy, egg producing or not egg producing. Attention is a bit harder to quantify and measure.

But despite these differences, the maturation of the online marketplace for attention closely mirrors the development of our hypothetical chicken marketplace. In a predigital advertising economy, local newspapers sold space on their pages to generate revenue. Most of the time, that space was purchased by businesses wishing to advertise goods and services. Like the island chicken farmer, the local newspaper sold its space to local businesses and organizations, and negotiated these deals on a bespoke basis.

But, as with chickens, this artisanal process for buying and selling attention is cumbersome at scale. Facebook serves an astronomically larger number of advertisements than a mid-twentieth-century local newspaper. It also has a vastly broader pool of potential advertisers, from massive companies promoting their latest product to a community group fundraising for the local marching band. Scale introduces the same pressures to the attention market that we saw in our hypothetical chicken market. In order to buy and sell attention across a vast number of players with very different needs, it becomes necessary to standardize what is being sold.

We need a Standard Chicken Lot for our attention market. The search for this standard rapidly reaches into the realm of the philosophical. Can we measure attention in a simple and reliable way? Can we break human attention down into discrete units that can be exchanged in a marketplace?

The advertising industry is deeply invested in answering these questions in the affirmative. In 1996, industry leaders formed the Internet Advertising Bureau (later renamed the Interactive Advertising Bureau, or IAB), a private consortium dedicated to developing the standards that enable the online advertising market to function.[39] In 2004, the IAB published its "Ad Impression Measurement

Guidelines," an initial set of foundational standards by
which an ad is considered "delivered" to a consumer by
the industry.[40]

The battles over these standard definitions have been
fierce, because they define the terms under which advertisers pay for online ads and how they measure their success. For instance, we might say an ad has been "delivered"
when it is successfully loaded up on a website. That definition has the advantage of being extremely easy to measure:
an ad server can log that it sent an ad, and the website
can confirm that the ad has been displayed. But assum-
ing this definition as the bar for success might massively
overreport the amount of attention that an ad is capturing.
What if the ad is loaded, but is buried in a place on the
website where no one ever sees it? Tons of ads could be
"successfully delivered" under this metric without reaching anyone.

We might try to raise the bar by only counting an ad
as "successfully delivered" when a user pauses on the ad
and actually looks at it for a period of time. But how long
do users need to pause on the ad? How can we verify that
they are looking at it? Setting the threshold for success
too high creates new problems—by defining the attention
asset so narrowly, we risk overly constraining the market. Publishers might end up with real attention they are
unable to sell because the standards for measuring and
verifying it are too stringent.

Much of the IAB's work focuses on building consensus
in answering these fundamental line-drawing questions:
the organization has brought together numerous working

groups that create and update guidelines specifying what constitutes a measurable blob of attention.

Like the standards for soybeans or corn, attention standards can be impressively specific. In 2014, the group released an extension of its 2004 work that standardized the concept of a "viewable impression." To achieve a viewable impression, more than 50 percent of the pixels in an advertisement must occupy the viewable space of a browser page for greater than or equal to one continuous second after the advertising renders.[41] The IAB specifies that "satisfying the minimum pixel requirement should precede the measurement of the time duration; for example, the clock starts on determining whether the ad meets the one continuous second time requirement only when the ad is determined to have met the 50% pixel threshold."[42] Numerous other standards define other aspects of the ad delivery process, from guidelines on the placement of an ad on the page to a commonly recognized set of formats for displaying an ad.[43]

The implications of this standardization effort are profound. Commodification enables a fluid marketplace. The amorphous, shapeless concept of attention has been transformed into discrete, comparable pieces that can be captured, priced, and sold. Buyers and sellers can quickly evaluate opportunities and transact in attention at massive scale, without individually evaluating each opportunity.

Standardization has made attention an abstract, economic asset as well. It is now possible to purchase attention in the marketplaces without knowing where and how that attention was produced. The idea is to enable the capture of a desired amount of attention at a minimum cost. As with standard units like "No. 1 Spring Corn" and the SCL, the modern programmatic advertising marketplace makes attention an interchangeable asset.

The commodification of attention in the 2000s created a fertile environment for market automation, something that was not possible in the Chicago grain markets of the 1850s. The industry definition of an impression is rigid and measurable, making impressions highly amenable to computerization. The existing infrastructure allows anyone to set up an advertiser account on an ad exchange and start buying and selling attention algorithmically with a global pool of willing counterparties. No special expertise or industry connections are required.

The overall impact of this seamless transacting and automation is obvious. In the same way that the standardization and automation of financial markets allowed those markets to explode in size and scope, so too has this standardizing process enabled digital advertising markets to see unprecedented growth in the last two decades.[44]

But commodification does more than allow buyers and sellers to transact more freely. It also gives rise to a set of incentives that can cause such marketplaces—under the right circumstances—to inherit some of the pathologies observed in financial markets over the past few decades. Now that it has adopted the form of these other marketplaces, a key question becomes whether online advertising, too, will face some of the same structural vulnerabilities.

Crisis on the Way?

In 2005, the economist Raghuram Rajan presented a paper at a private gathering of central bankers and economists in Jackson Hole, Wyoming. The paper was titled "Has Financial Development Made the World Riskier?"[45] Rajan made the prescient argument that certain changes in global finance—while producing a wide range of benefits—had also created perverse incentives that posed systemic risks to the integrity of the financial sector. At the time, this paper was derided by the former U.S. Treasury secretary Lawrence Summers as fundamentally unsound.[46] In hindsight, Rajan's diagnosis correctly identified many of the factors that produced the global financial crisis just a few years later.

Reading Rajan's paper more than a decade after the 2008 mortgage crisis, I find striking similarities between the transition that has taken place in the world of online advertising and the transition that took place in the financial markets during the 2000s. For example, Rajan describes a shift from transactions "embedded in a long-term relationship between a client and a financial institution" to transactions "conducted at arm's length in a market." He characterizes this shift as a "process of 'commodification' of financial transactions" driven by a combination of technological, regulatory, and institutional change.[47] For Rajan, this introduces a series of potentially risky incentives into the system, even as it spreads risk and expands participation in the financial markets.

Online advertising, too, has become increasingly com-

modified and "at arm's length" in its design. By and
large, long-term relationships do not characterize the
transactions that take place in the real-time bidding
systems for allocating advertising inventory. Programmatic advertising goes on without either party knowing
much about the other or having to interact person-to-
person at all. Indeed, the goal of dominant players like
Facebook and Google is to make buying attention on their
platforms as "self-serve" and automated as possible. As in
the financial markets, commodification has led to a massive increase in the size and interconnectedness of advertising markets and has allowed a much broader set of
actors to participate.

These rough parallels between advertising and finance
invite deeper exploration. Like Rajan, we might ask a simple question: Has the development of online advertising
made the world riskier? Are the unhealthy dynamics produced by commodification in the 2008 financial markets
mirrored in online advertising markets? Perhaps most
important, can we use the history of the financial markets as a guide to the future development of the internet's
economy?

To be sure, there are substantive differences between
financial markets and advertising. Advertising markets
involve bidding over the right to show something to someone. Advertising is consumed at the point it is acquired,
and its value is based on whether it shapes behavior in some
way. That might be as concrete as persuading someone to
make a purchase, or as abstract as improving someone's
opinion of the brand being promoted. In contrast, stocks

are bought and sold, and profit is derived from the difference in value between markets or over time. Buyers of advertising inventory generally do not "hold" ad space to sell at a higher value later (though attempts are being made to introduce these types of transactions in the marketplace).[48]

However, the mechanisms of a market crisis do not depend on these differences. As the economists Carmen Reinhart and Kenneth Rogoff write, "Financial crises follow a rhythm of boom and bust through the ages. Countries, institutions, and financial instruments may change across time, but human nature does not."[49] Reinhart and Rogoff catalog an entire bestiary of different financial crises, from governments defaulting on their debt to faltering promises to maintain an exchange rate. The specific kind of asset does not matter; a market crisis is ultimately a crisis of confidence.

A number of factors are handmaidens to the emergence of a full-blown market crisis. Market opacity plays a fundamental role. The inability to see what is actually happening within a marketplace allows doubt and panic about the value of an asset to set in. In the 2008 crisis, financial innovation in the form of collateralized debt obligations and complex options pricing algorithms prevented the players from having a clear idea of what was going on.[50] Past financial crises in markets around the world have shown that opaque government balance sheets and finances can also trigger doubt that escalates into panic.[51]

Opacity allows the value of the thing being bought and sold to deteriorate in secret, without anyone knowing.

In the subprime crisis of 2007–2008, packages of shoddy mortgages that were nearly certain to default at unexpectedly high rates were increasingly circulating in the marketplace. Opacity allowed these toxic assets to trade at prices far above what they were actually worth.

Opacity isn't dangerous only because it can cause errors in valuation. It also allows the active inflation of a market despite the fundamental shakiness of the thing being bought and sold. This sometimes results from irrational levels of market confidence, a regular feature of financial crises going back hundreds of years. Reinhart and Rogoff refer to the "this time is different" syndrome, in which "financial professionals and, all too often, government leaders explain that we are doing things better than before, we are smarter, and we have learned from past mistakes."[52]

But market inflation can also result from deliberate recklessness. Perverse incentives can emerge in a market, encouraging players to continue pushing the bright horizons for a marketplace despite knowing that major structural problems exist. Later reporting about the mortgage crisis illustrates the extent to which major financial actors were aware of the dangers but continued to participate anyway. In the infamous words of Chuck Prince, then the head of Citigroup, "When the music stops . . . things will be complicated. But as long as the music is playing, you've got to get up and dance. We're still dancing."[53]

Opaque markets, in short, allow expectations about a market to diverge from reality. On the one hand, things can get a whole lot worse without anyone knowing. On the other, conflicted players can overheat the market without being checked. This divergence between rosy outlooks and structural vulnerabilities is kindling for crises of confidence. When a hot, overpriced commodity is discovered to be effectively worthless, panic can set in, causing the market to implode.

Closely examining the state of the programmatic advertising marketplace makes it clear that these dynamics are very much in play in the economy of the web. The online attention marketplaces that underwrite the internet might have inherited not only the structure of modern financial markets but the pathologies of those markets as well. The seemingly endless growth of the modern-day advertising giants of the web may rest on shakier foundations than might initially appear.

3

Opacity

The advertising industry has long struggled with a simply stated but deeply complex question: Does advertising work? In other words, how does one really know that the advertising messages being broadcast actually influence the great mass of browsers, readers, and listeners out in the world? Traditionally, this struggle has been summed up by a pithy adage often attributed to John Wanamaker, an early advertising industry pioneer, who noted that "half the money I spend on advertising is wasted; the trouble is I don't know which half."[1]

To the outsider, this long-standing institutional ignorance can seem a bit puzzling. After all, one would think that making reasoned judgments about what types of advertising work and don't work is the primary job of the marketer, and the marketing industry as a whole.

It turns out that this is a much more difficult task than it might initially seem. Imagine you have to promote a new brand of cereal. You want lots of people to know about this new cereal, so you pay to put up a billboard right next to a busy highway. You might know roughly how many people pass by that billboard based on traffic statistics, but that doesn't tell you anything about who noticed the advertising, who was influenced by it, and whether it did anything for the cereal. You might find that cereal sales increased after the billboard went up, but how can you ever know whether the sales were due to that billboard? A person who saw the billboard and then later bought the cereal might have picked it up on a whim at the supermarket, or been persuaded to try it by a friend. There's simply no way to know whether the billboard played a role in the purchasing decision.

In contrast, online ads are traceable, trackable, and thoroughly quantified. This has been a selling point for digital advertising since the very beginning. Google's early nemesis GoTo—later renamed Overture—claimed in the early days of programmatic advertising that "[online advertising] is one of the few truly measurable media."[2] Google's then CEO, Eric Schmidt, would claim in 2008 as the AdWords product was taking off that the company's growing profits were attributable to its "system [being] better and more measurable than other forms of advertising."[3] Wanamaker's law appeared to have met its match.

The popular press covering the internet often echoed this opinion. In 1998, *Wired* magazine opined that "the Net is accountable. It is knowable. It is the highway leading marketers to their Holy Grail: single-sourcing technology that can definitively tie the information consumers perceive to the purchases they make."[4] This claim was repeated almost a decade later in 2006, when *The Economist* declared an end to the "Wanamaker era" of advertising, arguing that the internet was giving rise to a world where "advertisers pay only for real and measurable actions by consumers, such as clicking on a web link, sharing a video, placing a call, printing a coupon or buying something."[5]

That the internet affords a quantity of information inconceivable to earlier generations of advertisers is indisputable. A complex ecosystem of data brokers, tracking cookies, and surveillance now enables advertising to be precisely targeted, and the results of that advertising to be monitored. Today, an advertisement can be easily targeted to a specific audience defined by an incredibly granular set of characteristics, from race and gender to income and location. Ads delivered online can track how long the ad is viewed, when it is seen, and how soon people make a purchase after viewing it.

This monitoring infrastructure allows advertisers to accomplish feats of marketing that would have been prohibitively expensive or otherwise impossible in a pre-internet era. "Retargeting"—which identifies when a specific user has seen a product online, and delivers that user ads for the same product again and again as she browses the web—is possible because of the level of tracking that online advertising provides.[6] Computer security experts have shown that it is even possible to identify the location of a single, specific person using only the geotargeting infrastructure of commonplace programmatic advertising tools.[7] Our cereal billboard campaign is positively Stone Age, from a measurability standpoint.

Today's advertisers are flooded with data about consumers. If anything, they are struggling to figure out how to manage the tidal wave of data now available to them. It is technically feasible to know that *this* ad was viewed by *this* individual, at *this* time, in *this* location. It's even possible to know when and whether the individual purchased the advertised good or service.

Deeper context, however, remains elusive. Consumer behavior is exposed in fine detail, but the overall market stays opaque. The wealth of tracking data doesn't help advertisers determine a fair going price for reaching a particular kind of person, and buyers in the programmatic marketplace can have limited knowledge about where or how their ads will appear.

The measurability of the online ad economy is an inch wide and a mile deep. As such, the tidal wave of data that has accompanied the development of online advertising provides only an illusion of greater transparency.

This matters because opacity permits market bubbles to form. In the mortgage crisis, the complexity of the market in exotic financial instruments made it challenging to see that the underlying mortgages were extremely likely to default. If buyers had known that AAA-rated mortgage-backed securities contained so much bad debt, it would have been challenging to get anyone to buy the assets.[8]

Modern online advertising remains deeply opaque on three fronts. First is the ever-increasing automation of the marketplace. Second is the creation of dark pools of liquidity where advertising inventory is bought and sold outside the public eye. Third is the dominance of platforms, like Facebook and Google, that have frequently introduced new layers of opacity into the advertising marketplace.

I. Algorithmic Trading

Programmatic advertising delivers the vast number of ads that you see online today. In order to function, the entire system depends on a real-time auction between advertisers that takes place while a web page is loading. Making this real-time bidding (RTB) process seamless requires extreme speed.

Ad exchanges have achieved this speed through automation. Advertisers and publishers alike program systems that autonomously offer and price ad inventory in the marketplace. Advertisers can precisely define the kind of attention they would like to bid for, specifying audience parameters, maximum bid prices, timing, frequency, and certain kinds of inventory.[9] In turn, publishers can set minimum prices, rules for advertiser eligibility, and other preferences on the sale of their inventory.

This highly automated arrangement has allowed online advertising exchanges to deliver mind-bogglingly large quantities of inventory night and day, unceasingly. As in the financial markets, algorithmic trading has become the rule, rather than the exception.[10]

This blend of speed, automation, and scale has introduced new opacity into the marketplace even as it has allowed those marketplaces to substantially expand. The vast number of transactions taking place can make it impossible for anyone to monitor precisely where an ad ends up and why. This is a problem even for the professional buyers and sellers of ad inventory themselves. One *New York Times* investigation quoted Alex Treadway, then chief operating officer of the conservative website *The Daily Caller*, saying, "There is so much junk between us and the companies that buy ad space on our pages it will blow your mind . . . It would take us weeks of research to figure out which ad network provided [an] ad."[11]

Consider the chronic challenge posed by "brand safety"—the industry term for avoiding having advertisements show up next to objectionable content. YouTube has been the subject of multiple embarrassing news reports highlighting that brands advertising on the platform occasionally find their ads alongside extremist videos. In 2018, CNN reported that ads from more than three hundred companies on YouTube were placed next to channels that promoted "white nationalists, Nazis, pedophilia, conspiracy theories and North Korean propaganda."[12] This included major brands like Adidas, Hilton, and Hershey. This is not an isolated incident. The issue has been a longstanding concern among advertisers as the programmatic advertising ecosystem has matured over the past two decades.[13]

The persistence of this problem is not due to a lack of interest in resolving it. A survey in 2018 showed that brand safety was one of the top concerns among professionals within the industry, next to worries about "transparency" and the European Union's General Data Protection Regulation.[14] A 2017 survey of its members by the Association of National Advertisers found that 78 percent of respondents were "either concerned or very concerned about brand safety issues in programmatic buying."[15] The fact that brand safety remains an ongoing challenge even among platforms run by the most well-resourced companies in the world suggests how structural this opacity problem is.

To date, the primary approach has been to use human review in an effort to weed out these errors. The scale of the modern online advertising ecosystem makes this at best a partial solution. Mark Zuckerberg, commenting on Facebook's decision to hire more content moderators in 2017, declared, "No matter how many people we have on the team, we'll never be able to look at everything."[16] There is hope that recent advances in artificial intelligence might be able to ensure greater brand safety, but it is unclear whether these systems will ever have the context sufficient to address these issues in a comprehensive way. AI systems are able to recognize specific, concrete targets within images but remain extremely limited in understanding broader context. This makes AI a promising tool for dealing with problematic content where the boundaries of what is prohibited are clear, but a highly limited tool when dealing with more general categories of objectionable content.[17] AI will not serve as a cure-all to brand safety writ large.

In the programmatic advertising marketplace, it can be challenging to know where an ad will end up and why. This risk to brand safety pressures well-positioned buyers and sellers to look for safer ways to place ads online. This pressure, ironically, has introduced another compounding layer of opacity in the marketplace for online advertising.

II. Dark Pools

Not knowing where and why ads end up in the places that they do is a big problem. But in the attention marketplace, advertisers sometimes do not even know whose attention is available, much less the price that they should be paying.

"Dark pools" are a major phenomenon in the financial markets, accounting for some 14 percent of all equity volume traded in the United States.[18] These are, in effect, private stock markets run by investment banks and other financial institutions about which no public information is available. These structures ostensibly serve to allow buyers and sellers to execute large-scale transactions without triggering reactive fluctuations in price on public exchanges like the Nasdaq.

Dark pools are controversial in the financial sector because the opacity they create provides opportunities for abuse. When the public markets no longer reflect the supply and demand of all players, the prices shown on these exchanges will not reflect the actual value of the security. Dark pools enable practices like "front-running," in which high-frequency trading firms leverage their insider knowledge of these private marketplaces to profit off traders with slower access to information.[19]

It turns out that parallel structures have also emerged in the online advertising markets. Platforms increasingly give select buyers and sellers access to private marketplaces (PMPs)—exclusive exchanges for ad inventory. PMPs allow selected advertisers who have negotiated a special deal with a publisher to bid for advertising space, usually of a higher quality and in a less crowded, and therefore less competitive, market. These arrangements are attractive because they offer better transparency to the participants and also allow buyers to keep targeting data and other valuable information away from the public markets.[20]

PMPs are a growing segment of the transactions taking place in online advertising. In 2018, 45 percent of all the money spent in real-time bidding auctions took place within the confines of a PMP. Of the $19 billion that are projected to enter into the programmatic ad space between 2018 and 2020, the majority will go toward PMPs and other private arrangements.[21] By 2021, spending on PMPs is projected to exceed spending in open exchanges by more than $2 billion.[22] Ironically, this trend is driven by the opacity of public programmatic marketplaces, where brand safety and an overall lack of transparency make for a more risky advertising environment.

On a systemic level, PMPs introduce a new source of opacity while ameliorating the problem for a select few. If you lack access to a PMP, you cannot see the activity in these premium dark pools of advertising inventory. This introduces many of the same structural issues that accompany the rise of dark pools in the financial markets.

For one, the publicly available price no longer reflects the supply and demand across all the players in the marketplace. That means it is harder to know what the prevailing value of an ad is. Is the price paid to deliver an ad to a given consumer too much or too little relative to the overall market? Is a specific kind of ad receiving more demand over time, or is that demand falling?

Ambiguity about price reintroduces some of the challenges that programmatic advertising was intended to solve. By creating an interconnected set of markets with competitive bidding, programmatic advertising promised to foster price transparency in the marketplace. That is, players in the market would have a good sense of how the rest of the market was sizing up the opportunities to buy and sell attention. The growth of PMPs muddies the waters again.

Programmatic advertising makes it challenging to effectively track whose attention an advertiser is buying. The growing presence of PMPs creates a hazy landscape of pricing and available inventory for the ad buyer. But the opacity problem is not limited to PMPs alone. The highly consolidated nature of the programmatic advertising ecosystem itself contributes significantly to the murkiness of the internet's attention economy.

III. The New Intermediaries

The development of online programmatic advertising is often cast as a story of disintermediation. This is true to some extent. Traditionally, marketing agencies have played a major role in facilitating the interaction between advertisers and publishers. Programmatic advertising has supplanted this middleman role, allowing buyers and sellers of ads to transact directly. As a result, the gatekeeping role of agencies has eroded, and marketing agencies have struggled as "self-serve" programmatic marketplaces have grown.[23]

That is undoubtedly a positive story in some respects. Advertisers have more direct control over how their messages are distributed to the public and can choose how best to achieve their specific goals. Publishers are no longer beholden to marketing agencies, who long served as gatekeepers to major advertising dollars. In economic terms, disintermediation is a happy ending: costs should be lower overall, and supply should be able to meet the demands for advertising faster and more effectively.

This story overlooks one important point: the companies that brought about disintermediation have themselves become intermediaries in the advertising space. Google, Facebook, and major ad exchanges have huge sway over the rules of buying and selling ads because of their relative size and the high level of consolidation in the marketplace.

That consolidation increases market opacity. The availability of data about the state of the global online advertising marketplace is now dependent on the business decisions of a small number of platforms. The failure to disclose relevant information or the publishing of misleading information can severely distort the advertising markets.

One striking illustration is the subject of an ongoing lawsuit around claims that Facebook made in 2015 promoting the attractiveness of video advertising on its platform.[24] At the time, the company was touting online video—and the advertising that could be sold alongside it—as the future of the platform, noting that it was "increasingly seeing a shift towards visual content on Facebook."[25] Mark Zuckerberg argued publicly that "the vast majority of the content that people consume online will be video."[26] Facebook backed this push by tweaking its News Feed algorithm to promote video, directing huge amounts of traffic toward this type of content.[27]

The company's "pivot to video" encouraged publishers to invest heavily in the creation of more video content, often at the expense of existing staff. The effort also fed substantial industry hype about the value of video advertising on Facebook.[28]

But it turned out that Facebook overstated the level of attention being directed to its platform on the order of 60 to 80 percent. By undercounting the viewers of videos on Facebook, the platform overstated the average time users spent watching videos.[29] Facebook later admitted that several other key video advertising metrics were overstated.[30] Creative accounting has dogged other marketing metrics that Facebook has promoted. One analyst noted that Facebook claimed to be able to reach 25 million more eighteen- to thirty-four-year-olds in the United States than should exist according to the U.S. census.[31] Another report cast doubt on Facebook's claims about the performance of "Watch," its stand-alone video platform.[32]

These inconsistencies have led some to claim that Facebook deliberately misled the advertising industry, a claim that Facebook has denied.[33] Plaintiffs in a lawsuit against Facebook say that, in some cases, the company inflated its numbers by as much as 900 percent.[34] Whatever the reasons for these errors in measurement, the "pivot to video" is a sharp illustration of how the modern advertising marketplace can leave buyers and sellers beholden to dominant platform decisions about what data to make available.

As this book goes to press, the controversies sparked by these and other disclosures have made Facebook and Google more willing to voluntarily accept third-party auditing of their metrics.[35] Under these new arrangements, the Media Rating Council—an independent nonprofit founded in 1964 that provides third-party accreditation of media—is granted internal access by the platforms to confirm that the specific metrics they report to advertisers are legitimate.[36] This development marks the end of a protracted period in which Google and Facebook resisted suggestions that they accept more verification and accountability of the metrics they distribute.[37]

I'm skeptical that the platforms' newfound tolerance of oversight represents a structural change in the marketplace. These accountability measures leave the fundamental balance of power between the intermediaries and the markets they facilitate largely unchanged. Indeed, both Google and Facebook retain the ultimate power to decide precisely which third-party partners are permitted to verify and measure advertisements distributed on these platforms. This gives them tremendous practical leverage over the degree of scrutiny that they face. Even with the ongoing audits, advertisers' access to granular data about the overall programmatic advertising marketplace will remain limited.

Public pressure and the threat of losing major advertisers have forced the platforms to accept only a limited level of third-party verification. Such reluctance might not have been possible in a more competitive marketplace, where media buyers could easily shift to platforms that offered more transparency. Instead, advertisers face the unenviable choice of buying ads on the unverifiable assurances of the major platforms or giving up the huge audiences these companies command. In this sense, the highly concentrated market of online advertising itself increases opacity in the marketplace.

Why Opacity Matters

Opacity in the programmatic advertising markets can seem very much like an industry insider's problem. Why should we care about the degree to which advertisers can get data about advertising inventory? If anything, shouldn't we be glad that the market is perhaps more opaque than advertisers would like? Opacity limits the intrusiveness of advertising and perhaps in some marginal way helps to protect a modicum of privacy.

We should care because opacity is a key precondition for market failure. Opaque markets are ones in which participants cannot accurately assess the value of things being bought and sold. This can allow irrational exuberance to push the prices of things far above their real value. It can also allow the value of things to erode significantly without it being widely known. In both examples, expectations about the market diverge from reality. When these expectations come crashing down—whether in the value of online advertising or in the stability of mortgage-backed securities—panic sets in.

Granted, the infrastructure of online advertising provides more clarity in certain areas, especially when compared with earlier channels of advertising. There is an unprecedented level of information available about the performance of advertising once it has been delivered. How many times and when an ad has been seen, for instance, are standard, widely available metrics that would have been very expensive or impossible to acquire in the past.

But murkiness persists in critical areas. Algorithmic trading makes it challenging to assess where ads end up and who sees them. Dark pools obscure the real price of ads, allowing selected buyers and sellers access to more information and better opportunities to place ads unavailable to the rest of the market. Market concentration has made buyers and sellers beholden to data provided by a handful of major platforms, raising the barriers to acquiring verified information about ad quality. It is unclear whether the prices emerging from real-time bidding accurately reflect the value of advertising inventory across the entire market. It is unclear why the bidding algorithms behave the way they do. It is easy to get granular information about a given ad that you have placed, but far harder to get a sense of the overall marketplace.

We should care about opacity in the programmatic

advertising marketplace because it has a big role to play in determining the future of these marketplaces and the future of an internet that is dependent on ads as a primary source of revenue.

On its own, opacity doesn't create a financial crisis. Pre-internet advertising was highly limited in the metrics that were available about performance, but it grew substantially as a market over the course of the twentieth century. People wanted to buy ads, even in an information-poor environment. It is still challenging for the buyers of attention to assess the quality and effectiveness of the assets they are buying, even with today's wealth of attention-tracking data. But if the underlying attention purchased online remains high quality nonetheless, the market might remain sustainable.

Opacity merely sets up the circumstances for expectations to diverge from reality. To precipitate a market crisis, other forces must both erode the true underlying value of the assets being traded in the marketplace and wildly inflate their perceived market value. It is to those forces we now turn.

4

Subprime Attention

Opacity in a marketplace creates a smoke screen behind which an economic situation can deteriorate significantly without the broader market's becoming aware of it. The realization that the thing being bought and sold is *in fact* worth less than buyers and sellers believe shakes confidence and can produce widespread panic.

There are good reasons to believe that online advertising inventory is steadily decreasing in value over time. Two forces drive this erosion of value: structural shifts in what people pay attention to, and a massive global economy of fraud in the programmatic advertising marketplace. These trends are hidden by the murkiness of online advertising, as well as by a pattern of bad incentives that encourage ongoing efforts to pump up and hype the market.

Amid all the industry jargon, one can lose sight of advertising's ultimate objective: to shape the behavior or perceptions of the viewer in some way. For it to do this, a few factors have to be in play. The message being delivered should be relevant to the recipient. It should be delivered at the right time. Most fundamentally, the ad must capture the recipient's attention. If the ad is ignored, money spent delivering it is effectively wasted.

This is a long way of saying that advertising *packages* attention: it is not the attention itself. All an advertiser wins in an ad exchange auction is the right to display its content on a loading web page. When a demand-side platform (DSP) is programmed to seek out opportunities to reach a demographic like "males 18 to 24 living in the United States," it tells us whom the advertising will ideally reach, but not whether the people who actually see the ad will be persuaded, or even interested.

This divergence between the asset being bought—ad inventory—and the asset underlying it that defines its value—attention—directly parallels what happened to collateralized debt obligations (CDOs) during the 2007–2008 crisis.

CDOs were, in effect, bundles of mortgages. Financial institutions packaged together mortgages of differing risk and then sold the stream of payments coming from these loans as a single asset. But the CDOs were not the mortgages themselves, and each CDO in practice contained different bundles of mortgages taken by different homeowners in different places. One CDO might contain high-quality home mortgages that would reliably pay out over the entire lifetime of the loan, and an identical CDO might be filled with high-risk mortgages likely to default. In financial parlance, both CDOs and online advertising inventory are *derivatives*—they derive their value from an underlying asset. CDOs draw their value from the mortgages they contain; online ad inventory draws its value from the attention that it represents.

We can think about any unit of advertising—a banner

ad on a website or a billboard on the side of a highway—as a rough proxy for the collection of eyeballs that see it. In the same way that we might peel back a CDO to learn what mortgages it actually contains, we can peel back an ad and assess the quality of the attention that it captures.

When we do this, a twofold problem emerges. First, the value of the attention "packaged" by online advertising is declining. Online advertising is increasingly ignored—or actively resisted—by the public at large. Second, the "attention" that ads do receive is increasingly garbage—the product of a massive, fraudulent economy designed to extract money from advertisers.

Attention is subprime. The bottom is falling out even as prices are pushed higher and higher. This is made possible and exacerbated by the pervasive opacity of the marketplace, which allows real value and market value to drift further apart over time.

Who's Paying Attention?

South Park is a pretty neighborhood located in the SoMa district of San Francisco. Set away from the busy, loud urban streets that bound the area, the neighborhood is built around a small oval park with a playground. It's home to a collection of startups, marketing agencies, venture capital firms, and very expensive apartments. There's a craft brewery, an artisan coffee shop, and a high-end grilled-cheese restaurant within a block of the park.

South Park is a significant location in the lore of San Francisco technology. The initial idea for Twitter was reputedly sketched out in the South Park playground, and the neighborhood was home to many leaders of the first dot-com boom.[1] But, beyond being a hub for product innovations that would shape the web, South Park is historically important for the role it plays in the broader development of the web as a business.

It was here in late 1994 that the online advertising economy was born. Two South Park was then home to HotWired, a subsidiary of *Wired* magazine that owned and operated the publication's website.[2] In partnership with Volvo, AT&T, and other major brands, HotWired launched the web's first banner ads.

The early banner ads of the mid-1990s were wildly successful compared with the ads of today. One common ad industry benchmark for success is the click-through rate, which measures the percentage of people viewing the ad who subsequently clicked on the ad. In other words, just how compelling was an ad to given users that they went out of their way to click on that ad to learn more?

The information we have suggests that this early generation of ads captured attention in a way that is virtually unheard-of today. When they launched in 1994, the first banner ads generated a remarkable click-through rate of 44 percent.[3] That is, close to half of the people who saw these banners clicked on them. Today, banner ads command far less attention. One data set drawn from Google's ad network suggests that the average click-through rate for a comparable display ad in 2018 was 0.46 percent. For some industries, that number is as low as 0.39 percent.[4] That's about one in every two hundred people. Recent attempts to measure click-through rates on Facebook ads reveal similar rates of less than 1 percent.[5]

These banner-type ads are a hundred times less effective than they were about twenty-five years ago. Even these sub-1-percent click-through rates may overstate the effectiveness of ads on some platforms. On mobile devices, close to 50 percent of all click-throughs are not users signaling interest in an advertisement, but instead accidental "fat finger" clicks—users unintentionally clicking on content while using a touch-screen device.[6] Ads may also drive a response among only a small segment of the population. In 2009, one study estimated that 8 percent of internet users were responsible for 85 percent of all advertisement click-throughs online.[7]

Public indifference toward online ads is reflected in the surprisingly ambiguous empirical evidence that these ads do anything at all. One large-scale experimental study of online search ads in 2014 concluded that "brand-keyword ads have no measurable short-term benefits." Ironically, ads generated engagement mostly among "loyal customers or [consumers] otherwise already informed about the company's product." The ads, in other words, were an expensive way of attracting users who would have purchased anyway, leading to "average returns that are negative."[8]

This indifference toward advertising is particularly pronounced among younger internet users. In 2013, a controlled experiment on more than a million customers to evaluate the causal effect of online ads concluded that a customer "between ages 20 and 40 experienced little or no effect from the advertising." This was in spite of this demographic's proportionally heavier usage of the internet. In contrast, the study found that customers older than sixty-five, despite constituting only 5 percent of the experimental group, were responsible for 40 percent of the total effect observed as a result of the advertising.[9] This result suggests that the current effectiveness of advertising may depend on an aging and rapidly disappearing segment of the population.

Skeptical minds might counter that click-throughs and sales are imperfect proxies for measuring whether ads are effective. Marketers frequently draw a distinction between "direct response" advertising and "brand" advertising. The former encourages an audience to make a purchase—by promoting a discount, for instance, or highlighting the attractive features of a product. "Brand" advertising, in contrast, is less about the immediate purchase and more about shaping the public's associations with a brand and differentiating it from its competitors. Nike might invest in television advertising that is—at least in the near term—less intended to make consumers go out and buy sneakers and more intended to ensure that Nike maintains its status as a "cool" brand in the public eye. In brand advertising, clicks and sales are secondary to the advertiser's goal. Even if the ability of advertising to drive clicks and sales is falling over time, there might be enough demand in brand advertising to ensure that the value of online advertising inventory remains sound.

The vaporous nature of brand advertising means that the goalposts are perpetually moving: the objective of the advertiser may not be to drive any behavioral change that

is actually measurable in any sensible time frame. It becomes hard to refute the effectiveness of advertising when
the bar is set so low. But one thing is certain even in the
brand advertising context: if the ad is never delivered in
the first place, there is no way that it can be effective.
Industry trends suggest that this is precisely what is happening in the programmatic ecosystem.

The first problem is the ineffectual placement of ads
on pages. The real-time bidding system might successfully load up an ad on a website, but there is no guarantee
that the ad will be somewhere that a reader of the website
will actually see. Ads might load at the bottom of the page
outside the browser view, for instance, or they might be
so small that they escape notice entirely. "Ad viewability,"
as it is known in the industry, has emerged as a major
concern. In 2014, Google released a report suggesting
that 56.1 percent of all ads displayed on the internet are
never seen by a human.[10] One 2017 report by Comscore
found that this problem is particularly pronounced for
ads purchased through the programmatic ecosystem.[11] A
staggering number of those ads are never seen by anyone
at all.

But the problem goes deeper than bad placement. Not
only are people paying less attention to ads; they are also
taking proactive steps to prevent ads from reaching them
in the first place. Ad blocking grows more popular every
year. One study by Deloitte from 2017 suggests that fully
three-quarters of North Americans engage in "at least one
form of regular ad blocking."[12] In 2016, 615 million devices around the world were actively blocking ads.[13]

The news for advertisers gets even worse. Trends suggest that the industry is not even able to evade highly blocked markets by delivering ads to less blocked places. Markets outside North America, where ad blocking was historically less prevalent, might have been a potential haven for advertisers. But ad-blocking growth is particularly pronounced in these emerging markets. Driven largely by the growth of ad blocking in Asia-Pacific, global ad blocking grew by about 30 percent year over year from 2015 to 2016.[14]

Mobile platforms might also have been a promising new frontier, given their relative growth compared to desktop devices and the lack of norms around ad blocking on mobile devices. But it turns out that mobile is where ad blocking has grown the most in the past few years. Ad blocker use on mobile devices grew by 40 percent to 380 million devices between 2015 and 2016. Fifty-nine percent of the smartphones in India implement ad blocking.[15]

The full economic impact of ad blocking worldwide is huge. Adobe estimated in 2015 that $21.8 billion in global ad revenue is lost each year to ad blockers.[16] That's a significant annual loss, more than all the revenue generated by Facebook that year.[17] Relatively wealthier consumers also disproportionately adopt ad-blocking tools, reducing advertisers' access to some of the most valuable audiences on the web.[18] Generationally, the long-term trend is also worrisome. Ad blocking is significantly more prevalent in users eighteen to twenty-four than among older cohorts.[19] Since younger users also pay less attention to ads, the advertising industry may be facing a demographic shift in behavior that will dramatically erode the viability of its existing model.

The seriousness of the threat posed by ad-blocking software to the online advertising sector can be measured by the vitriol with which representatives of the industry have responded. Randall Rothenberg, who leads the IAB, declared melodramatically that ad blocking is "robbery, plain and simple—an extortionist scheme that exploits consumer disaffection and risks distorting the economics of democratic capitalism."[20]

It is worth recognizing that these arguments are about the aggregate trend of the online advertising economy. *Some* online advertising works, in *certain* contexts, for *particular* products. A close look at programmatic advertising does, in fact, reveal certain domains in which advertising remains highly effective. Famously, mesothelioma—the cancer caused by asbestos that has produced an active industry of class action lawsuits—remains one of the most expensive keywords to advertise against in search results, in part because people searching for this rare disease are in extreme need and are seeking treatment.[21]

But such domains are the exception, rather than the norm. Undermined by visibility problems, indifference, and ad blocking, online advertising overall is increasingly subprime. It fails to truly capture attention or influence consumer behavior. And it gets worse. As the quality of real attention on offer declines, fraudsters continuously work to inflate the value of the attention inventory being

sold. This poses a problem that, unchecked, could destabilize the economy of the web.

The Problem of Ad Fraud

The sheer size of the online advertising market invites attempts to fraudulently extract money from it. Exploitation
is rampant in the online advertising ecosystem. Perversely,
these activities actually boost the perceived value of advertising inventory—at least in the short term.

The basic idea of ad fraud is simple: buyers think they
are purchasing attention and delivering their message to
promising consumers, but instead they are given something worthless. There are numerous ways that this can
happen.

Click fraud is a widespread practice that uses automated scripts or armies of paid humans in "click farms"
to deliver click-throughs on an ad. The result is that the
advertising captures no real attention for the marketer. It
is shown either to a human who was hired to click on the
ad or to no one at all.

The scale of this problem is enormous. A study conducted by Adobe in 2018 concluded that about 28 percent
of website traffic showed "non-human signals," indicating
that it originated in automated scripts or in click farms.[22]
One study predicted that the advertising industry would
lose $19 billion to click fraud in 2018—a loss of about
$51 million per day.[23] Some place this loss even higher.
One estimate claims that $1 of every $3 spent on digital
advertising is lost to click fraud.[24]

Display advertising, which still constitutes one of the largest segments of the digital advertising market, exhibits these problems in a particularly striking way. In 2017, Forrester Research concluded that the previous year, as much as 56 percent of all ad dollars spent on display advertising were lost to fraudulent or otherwise unviewable inventory. This accounted for $7.4 billion of waste, which was estimated to grow to $10.9 billion by 2021.[25]

There is good reason to believe that fraud will continue to destabilize the industry, even as advertisers find new ways of delivering marketing messages through the web. Video, one of the fastest-growing segments of the programmatic advertising market, is similarly plagued by fraudulent traffic. Fraud accounts for 22 percent of video spend, and 20 percent of nonmobile video traffic is driven by bots. If anything, the problem is worse in video than it is in display. One study concluded that fraud was twice as common in video traffic as in display traffic.[26] Mobile, another quickly growing segment, is likewise vulnerable to fraud. Eighty-seven percent of all mobile devices on offer in the programmatic advertising markets in the United States in fall 2016 were fraudulent, meaning that they were either not real phones at all, or they were phones running automated scripts, unseen by any actual members of the public.[27]

Domain spoofing is another popular scam, in which inventory on the programmatic marketplace is made to look like space on a high-value website when it, in fact, is not. Unwitting ad buyers pay top dollar for these opportunities, not realizing that their ads appear somewhere else entirely. In 2017, the *Financial Times* discovered that fraudsters were pretending to sell *Financial Times* ad inventory on ten different ad exchanges. In fifteen ad exchanges, they also found offers to sell video advertising on the *Financial Times* site, a type of inventory the newspaper didn't even offer its legitimate advertisers. The fake inventory was selling for approximately $1.3 million per month, which the advertising operations director for the publication called "jaw-dropping."[28]

Ad fraud flourishes because it is highly lucrative. In 2018, *The New York Times* profiled one "entrepreneur" in the space, Martin Vassilev, who in eighteen months went "from being on welfare and living with his father in Canada to buying a white BMW 328i and a house of his own." Small operators delivering fake YouTube views with software can earn more than $30,000 per month.[29]

Ad fraud also supports the development of more sophisticated criminal enterprises that can target established publishers and even threaten the Google-Facebook duopoly. These advanced operators leverage malicious code to direct the traffic of unknowing consumers to support these ad fraud schemes. In 2018, a *BuzzFeed* story exposed a $10 million scheme that used more than 125 Android apps and website ads to generate fake traffic.[30] Methbot, a "professionalized" ad fraud scheme uncovered in 2016, generated between $3 million and $5 million per day at its height by impersonating inventory on nearly six thousand publications including *The Economist*, ESPN, *Fortune*, and Facebook.[31]

The vast cumulative impact of fraud in the programmatic advertising ecosystem is worth taking a moment to put in everyday terms. Imagine a supermarket with the level of inventory fraud that exists in the programmatic marketplace. In some aisles, one out of every five products on the shelves is a fake: you'd return home to find that these boxes contain nothing.[32] Even when you stick to familiar brands that you recognize and trust—a six-pack of Coca-Cola or a box of Wheaties—your purchases turn out to be imitations filled with sawdust. You'd probably stop going to this supermarket, even if you did occasionally manage to get some of the groceries you wanted.

The perverse effect of ad fraud in the short and medium term is that it actually inflates the purported value of the global marketplace for digital advertising. Fake traffic driven by click farms and botnets makes ads look better and more effective than they actually are. Practices like domain spoofing expand the apparent supply of opportunities to get an advertising message to high-value audiences. These fraudulent practices juice demand for online advertising and pump up the overall size of the marketplace.

All the while, ad fraud erodes the true value of the underlying attention inventory. As fraud spreads, a larger and larger proportion of the dollars spent on advertising fails to capture any real or worthwhile attention. Fraudulent practices also erode trust, because any real attention captured through these channels becomes more and more suspect. How is an advertiser to know that someone actually saw the ad that it paid to place? An expanding gap appears between the market price of advertising and the true value of the asset. Pervasive fraud contributes to online advertising's becoming increasingly subprime, capturing a declining proportion of real attention and an increasing proportion of fake attention.

Defusing the Crisis?

The problems of declining attention, ad blocking, and fraud that we have discussed are well-known within the programmatic advertising industry. They all represent structural threats to the continued growth and vitality of the online advertising markets and have been treated as such by the sector. This has led to a variety of attempts to intervene and fix the ecosystem, though it is far from clear whether these efforts have been effective in changing the overall picture.

Companies responsible for purchasing large quantities of advertising increasingly scrutinize their marketing agencies and demand greater accountability.[33] Buyers have pressured big platforms like Facebook and Google to allow more extensive third-party involvement in assessing the veracity of ad performance metrics.[34]

Technological solutions have also been developed. Introduced in 2017, ads.txt is one standard endorsed by the IAB to combat the problems of domain spoofing. The IAB encourages publishers to host a text file on their web servers containing an authoritative list of the sellers with permission to sell their inventory.[35] At least in theory, this would allow buyers to assess whether a vendor on a programmatic exchange is engaging in domain spoofing. Driven by enthusiastic adoption from Google, ads.txt use has risen sharply; among the top thousand sites selling programmatic ads, 57 percent now host these reference files.[36]

The fight to save the structure of online advertising also means fighting ad-blocking software. The advertising industry has worked to erode the effectiveness of ad blockers.[37] This is sometimes facilitated by the ad blockers themselves, who monetize their software by charging a premium to advertisers in exchange for access to people who block ads. Adblock Plus—one of the most popular companies operating in the space—launched its Acceptable Ads Platform in 2016, effectively creating a new ad network through which advertisers meeting certain criteria could access the ad blocker's user base.[38]

The other approach taken by the advertising industry has been to grow past the problem. Rather than take on the daunting task of repairing existing marketplaces plagued by fraud and subprime attention, the strategy is to expand programmatic advertising into new media where it might capture higher-quality attention. The expansion into video, mobile platforms, and games reflects a strategy to create an alternative that might allow the industry to dump the existing workhorse of display advertising.

Despite these multifaceted efforts, the fundamentals have not changed. Ad fraud continues to be a cat-and-mouse battle. When old vulnerabilities are patched up, fraudsters find new ways to extract money illegitimately from the marketplace. The net effect is that fraud in these channels is not only persistent, but on the rise. One industry analysis suggests that ad fraud will more than double in the coming years, eventually reaching $44 billion by 2022, an amount equivalent to about 9 percent of the overall digital ad spend.[39]

Tactics like domain spoofing remain effective even with the advent of tools like ads.txt. One 2018 report showed that while ads.txt did lower the rate of fraud, the overall rate remained high.[40] Even supposedly "safe" domains still saw fraud in excess of 13 percent.[41] Fraudsters are nimble in this new environment; nothing about ads.txt prevents the introduction of fraudulent entities to individual websites' "approved" lists. Publishers have been threatened and tricked into adding suspicious names to their lists.[42] A scheme uncovered by researchers in 2018 specifically targeted vulnerabilities of the ads.txt program and could have cost the industry $70 million to $80 million had it gone unchecked.[43]

Nor has continued innovation to grow past the problem proven to be a particularly promising solution. Advertising in online video or through mobile platforms remains a relatively small sliver of the digital ad market. Neither is currently positioned to generate enough ad revenue to supplant search or display advertising. At the same time, many of these new channels suffer from the same problems of fraud, sometimes at even greater rates than before.

Mobile ad fraud is "surging"; by some estimates it doubled in 2017.[44]

And always lurking in the background is the specter of a public uninterested in online advertising. The adoption of ad-blocking programs continues to rise globally, with particularly rapid adoption on mobile devices.[45] This accompanies evidence that younger cohorts of internet users pay less and less attention to ads on new platforms. Snapchat—which has a disproportionately young user base—has been plagued by the fact that its users reliably "skip commercial interruptions within less than a second."[46] One 2017 survey of eighteen- to thirty-five-year-olds shows that fully 59 percent watch online video ads only until they can skip them, and another 11 percent block ads entirely.[47]

Past performance is, of course, no indication of future returns. The advertising industry might identify new ways of delivering ads online that can scale and capture attention at the same levels the original banner advertisements did in the 1990s. It might triumph in the long term over ad blockers and the scams that currently erode value in the advertising marketplace. Achieving these goals would require massive coordination between players in the programmatic marketplace and more than a few painful compromises.

There are real reasons to doubt that the market's structural weaknesses will be corrected. Financial crises, as we have seen, can emerge even when players in the market know the risks of a growing bubble or the underlying weakness of a widely hyped asset. People who know the dangers of an overheated market and who have the ability to change it are seldom able to stem the tide of a crisis—in the rare cases when they try at all. The online attention markets of the web are exhibiting similar qualities, raising the question: What allows a bubble to keep growing, and what might cause it to pop?

5

Inflating the Bubble

Opacity and subprime attention create the necessary conditions for a market bubble in online advertising. This chapter examines how this dysfunctional market might grow overheated and then suddenly implode.

Granted, the advertising industry may resolve its many structural issues before a market crisis comes to pass. Optimists point to recent attempts to address fraud and wean people from ad blocking. They argue that it is still early for emerging channels like video and that many problems of inattention will be ironed out over time. These hypothetical changes to the industry might slowly let the air out of a bubble, preventing a sudden, damaging crash. However, these efforts would need to be effective in a way that they haven't been to date.

Just because a problem is known doesn't mean that it will be solved in time. The history of financial crises shows numerous situations in which buyers, sellers, and the companies running the markets failed to take sufficient action to avert a market bubble. That history has lessons here.

Two complementary factors are important. On the demand side, there needs to be a flow of cash into a marketplace that inflates a bubble in spite of the market-place's structural weaknesses. On the supply side, various players need to benefit from this flow of money. It becomes in their financial interest to disregard warning signs, limit structural changes, and keep the market growing even as alarm bells ring. Perverse incentives of this kind were a central cause of the 2008 subprime mortgage crisis and are present in the modern online advertising ecosystem today.

The Cash Bubble

Why aren't advertisers more wary of all the structural issues that we've discussed? The murkiness of the programmatic advertising market and the challenges of subprime attention are well-known, but advertisers continue, quarter after quarter, to pump money into the digital ad economy.

One might argue that this continued investment means that these problems don't pose a serious threat to the integrity of the overall market—that people are, in effect, signaling their confidence with their dollars. Parallels to past crises in financial markets offer an alternate hypothesis: advertising budgets are pouring into this market bubble because they have nowhere else to go. Let's return to the subprime mortgage crisis for an illustrative example.

One prevailing thesis about the origins of the 2008 crisis is known among economists as the "savings glut" hypothesis. This theory observes that fiscal instability in the 1990s encouraged developing countries around the turn of the twenty-first century to aggressively shift their money into safe assets. This process triggered a wave of purchases of U.S. Treasuries—debts of the U.S. government—by countries like China. U.S. Treasuries are widely considered the safest investments available, given that they are backed by the credit of the United States.

The scale of this shift toward safe investments was massive. Between 1996 and 2003, developing countries as a group shifted about $293 billion in this way, changing from net importers of capital (that is, bringing money from other countries into their country) to massive net exporters of capital (sending money to other countries).[1] Much of that money ended up in the United States. The U.S. Financial Crisis Inquiry Commission, which was responsible for investigating the origins of the 2008 crisis, would later note that "from 2000 to 2006, U.S. Treasury debt held by foreign official public entities rose from $0.6 trillion to $1.43 trillion; as a percentage of U.S. debt held by the public, these holdings increased from 18.2% to 28.8%."[2]

The savings glut hypothesis suggests that this massive shift in the movement of money created the circumstances for a broader crisis. Demand for these safe assets was so ravenous that the price of U.S. Treasuries rose, driving down their overall return. This prompted foreign investors and financial institutions to seek out new alternatives—assets that were just as safe but with higher returns. Securitized mortgages, with their reputation for stable growth over the long term, seemed like an ideal solution.

Mortgage originators were incentivized to make riskier and riskier subprime loans as the demand for these assets continued to grow. As a percentage of all mortgages, subprime mortgages rose from 8 percent of the market in 2003 to 20 percent in 2005.[3] Those mortgages would go bust en masse, eventually triggering the broader financial crisis.

The key lesson of the savings glut hypothesis is that large flows of money seeking safe harbors can produce the conditions for a bubble to form. After decades of financial instability, governments in the developing world sought safe places to put their money. As the price of the safest option—U.S. government debt—rose, mortgages appeared to many financial institutions to offer an ideal combination of affordability and reliability. Those structural flows drove the market up even as warning signs began to emerge that the mortgages being issued were nowhere near as stable as was originally thought.

The savings glut hypothesis is controversial. Some argue that it understates the failure of financial regulators to address the warning signs that presaged a broader crisis. The journalist Martin Wolf says the hypothesis "may have had the right analysis, but the Fed's was the wrong response, made worse by the failure to regulate the financial system."[4] Like many complex social and economic phenomena, no single cause brought about the 2008 subprime crisis. However, as we think about online advertising markets and their fragility, the savings glut hypothesis provides a provocative argument for explaining why ad markets may continue to grow despite their known weakness.

We have been diving deep into the programmatic advertising marketplace for the last few chapters, but it is worth thinking about the broader landscape that an ad buyer faces. The ad buyer has to distribute a limited budget as effectively as possible across the various channels available to her. This might involve buying ads through the methods we've been focused on: bidding to distribute ads through platforms like Facebook and Google, or buying an ad through an exchange. But it might also include older, established media: buying an ad in a newspaper, or arranging for a television spot, or renting billboards in major cities around the country.

All of these channels provide a certain level of perceived return to the ad buyer. This might be measured in extremely concrete ways—purchases of a product—or in softer ways that reflect a more brand-advertising-based approach. An advertiser might find it valuable to expose a product to an audience that is unfamiliar with it, regardless of the immediate purchases they choose to make. The ad buyer is an investor of a sort, choosing how to allocate limited resources across many different types of promotions that offer different kinds of returns.

In this context, online platforms like Facebook and Google offer new, shiny assets in the broader marketplace for grabbing attention. Google and Facebook do not simply compete with one another for ad dollars; they also compete against the many other kinds of businesses that offer slices of attention for a fee. Digital advertising is just one kind of investment in the marketplace for attention. Ad buyers can choose to spend their limited dollars on digital instead of, say, television, hoping for a greater proportional return.

And for the most part, they have done just that. The meteoric growth of online advertising has come at the expense of traditional attention channels.[5] Classified ads, the old advertising workhorse that funded many a local newspaper, were outcompeted by platforms like Craigslist and Google.[6] Globally, digital ads are a $273 billion business, but this is just a subset of the bigger industry of advertising. Overall ad spending across all media in 2018 was $629 billion. Digital is, however, poised to take over more and more of that overall amount, and in 2019 projections showed that fully half of all ad spending would go to digital by 2020.[7]

Digital companies see a future in extracting the advertising dollars still currently invested in older, established channels for distributing messages. This explains in part Facebook's pivot to video and Google's continued investment in YouTube. The successful capture of even part of the money that is spent on television ads would bring in billions for these platforms.[8]

But this is a two-sided game. Facebook and Google do not just compete with television networks and billboard companies for the dollars that advertisers are looking to spend. They are competing with these other advertising channels for public attention, too. The internet captures some of the finite attention that other media channels are vying for as well. People can watch YouTube instead of broadcast television or choose to read blogs over newspapers.

This makes digital advertising a double threat. On the one hand, digital advertisers compete against other media channels for advertising dollars. Coca-Cola, for instance, might choose to put advertising dollars into promoting its latest soft drink on Facebook rather than airing a commercial on CNN. On the other hand, digital advertisers also compete for the viewers that make legacy media channels attractive to advertisers in the first place. Consumers increasingly spend time on Facebook that they might otherwise spend watching CNN. Facebook thus appears more valuable to the advertiser. As advertisers give less money to media like newspapers, they also cripple the ability of newspapers to offer the content that subscribers demand. This makes it harder for legacy media companies to compete against their digital rivals.

This structural shift has far-reaching implications. Consider for a moment what effect this death spiral of legacy media has on ad buyers. It is not just that established media options are less attractive but that over the medium to long term they are increasingly unavailable as options at all.

The movement of consumers to digital platforms makes it riskier and less attractive for ad buyers to buy into anything but digital advertising. The shift of advertising dollars onto online platforms accelerates the deterioration and disappearance of competing outlets for distributing ads. The disappearance of those competing outlets, in turn, accelerates the flow of money onto online platforms. Increasingly, all roads lead to the programmatic advertising economy.

This structural shift looks a lot like the savings glut. Like developing world governments in the 1990s and early 2000s, advertisers confront a media ecosystem where traditional media outlets are looking shaky or are disappearing outright. This produces a huge influx of cash into the online advertising marketplace that has nowhere else to run. Some of that cash will end up in relatively safe places: the U.S. Treasuries of the online advertising world. Some of it will not, particularly as the limited number of safe, high-value opportunities rise in price and disappear into private marketplaces.

Under these circumstances, it would be difficult for the online advertising ecosystem to correct itself even if it had the will to do so. Ad buyers are unlikely to cut their budgets significantly even as the number of options for placing those budgets declines. That provides sufficient fuel for a bubble, despite the persistent problems of opacity and subprime attention.

But feeding that immense level of demand can also take on some perverse characteristics. Loan originators creating mortgages to meet global demand during the 2000s eventually found themselves under intense pressure to look the other way as the quality of those mortgages became shoddier and shoddier. Similarly, the marketing agencies and ad technology companies profiting most handsomely from these developments have few incentives to address the market's deep structural flaws. In some cases, they may even exacerbate these issues.

Perverse Incentives in Financial Markets

Online advertising inventory is increasingly dubious, whether it is ignored, blocked, or entirely fake. But a decline in value is not, in itself, a problem for a well-functioning marketplace. Buyers can simply refuse to pay a premium for online ads, driving the price of ad inventory downward. While the total value of advertising sold in the marketplace would decline, the market wouldn't necessarily implode dramatically. Prices can be a powerful means of averting market crisis. The market simply incorporates the risks of things like ad blocking and the generally lower level of attention paid to display inventory, and life goes on.

But if price fails to reflect reality, the price of the ads being bought and sold will remain stable as the real value of the underlying asset—attention—erodes. That raises the risk that these prices might suddenly "snap" to their real value amid a loss of confidence in what is being bought and sold.

How might this happen? We've already talked about one way. Market opacity can cripple the ability of price to accurately reflect value. Simply stated, if it's impossible to see the underlying assets in a marketplace, it is impossible for the market to price those assets accurately.

Another major contributing factor are the players in the marketplace. A potent brew of greed and insulation from consequences can encourage players to stoke the market and overvalue what is being traded. A critical mass of these bad actors will inflate the bubble and prevent the market from adjusting effectively over time. The record of the 2008 mortgage crisis is replete with examples of banks and rating agencies that took reckless bets and hid the true vulnerabilities of underlying assets.

On the bank side, mortgage-backed securities were traded on an "originate and distribute" basis, which meant that the institutions responsible for creating these assets did not hold them on their balance sheets. Instead, these assets were sold off into the marketplace, where they were traded among a large number of buyers and sellers. Because the originating banks were compensated by volume, bankers had perverse incentives to originate and package as many assets as possible to meet demand. In response to this pressure, banks began issuing mortgages to everyone who applied. Infamously, borrowers were able to obtain high levels of financing for purchasing homes with little money down and with no information required about their job or finances—so-called NINJA (no income, job, or assets) mortgages.[9]

As the market for mortgage-backed securities grew, the assets were increasingly filled with highly toxic, low-quality mortgages that were unlikely to ever be paid back. This problem was compounded by the Big Three of global credit ratings agencies—Standard & Poor's, Moody's, and Fitch Ratings—which were responsible for assigning grades to the packaged securities. The investment banks issuing these assets paid the ratings agencies, perversely incentivizing the agencies to give the banks' toxic mortgages high AAA ratings.[10] The high ratings fueled the market for these assets and obscured the real, underlying fragility of mortgage-backed securities. AAA ratings also enabled massive money market and pension funds, restricted from holding lower-rated assets, to purchase mortgage-backed securities in great numbers.

The incentive to overvalue mortgage-backed securities laid the groundwork for a larger crisis, because it was impossible to hide the underlying weakness of these assets indefinitely. Many of the mortgages packaged into these securities came with a "balloon rate" that would rapidly increase the interest due on the mortgages a few years after issuance. As these triggered in increasingly large numbers between 2006 and 2009, $738 billion in mortgages suffered "payment shock" and default.[11] The increase in mortgage failures cast doubt on the purported value of these assets, eventually triggering a widespread panic.

Similar conflicts pervade the modern marketing ecosystem, spurring the expansion of the programmatic market bubble even as the problems continue to grow. Marketing agencies and advertising technology companies play the role of the pre-crisis ratings agencies and loan originators. The business practices of these entities juice the market in ways that assist the growth of a bubble.

Perverse Incentives: Agencies and Ad Tech

Market bubbles are seldom a surprise to everyone. Industry insiders can buoy the growth of a marketplace even as the underlying fundamentals grow worse and worse. In the 2008 crisis, financial institutions and ratings agencies profited from the ever-expanding demand for mortgage-backed securities even while they were aware that the market was more fragile than it looked from the outside.[12]

In the online advertising marketplace, two groups have systemic incentives to oversell the value and price of advertising inventory regardless of issues like fraud, declining attention, and ad blocking. There are the marketing agencies, seeking profits in an increasingly unfriendly business environment. And there are the marketplaces themselves, which will cease to be profitable if people stop buying and selling online attention. These actors work to prop up the price of digital advertising inventory in spite of its eroding value.

The Agencies

Marketing agencies have long played an influential role as the middlemen between buyers and sellers of advertising inventory. This privileged role has come under competitive pressure in recent years as the rise of programmatic marketplaces has facilitated a more direct ecosystem of transactions between advertisers and publishers.[13] Functions previously tasked to agencies are now performed by other actors. For instance, creative development of advertising content has increasingly been brought in-house. Large advertisers have built their own internal agencies, and major publishers like Facebook and Google provide creative services directly to large advertisers.[14]

Financial pressure from clients is also rising. Clients are closely scrutinizing their return on investment and demanding greater transparency. From 2015 to 2018, major brands—including Shell, HSBC, and Mars—undertook top-to-bottom reviews of their marketing budget allocation.[15] This wave of budget reviews led to the cancellation of many long-standing contracts between clients and marketing agencies.[16] Marketing agencies face ever-shrinking profit margins in light of this loss of market position. This has left agencies scrambling to find other ways of making money in this new environment.

One controversial means of doing so is manipulating the price of advertising inventory through an industry practice known as arbitrage. Marketing agencies sign deals for discounted prices for ad inventory from publishers. These agencies then turn around and resell this inventory at a higher price to their clients, pocketing the difference. Similar practices exist in the acquisition and selling of consumer data by agencies to advertiser clients.[17]

Arbitrage is a major concern in the advertising industry because it potentially places the agency in conflict with the advertiser it supposedly represents. For one, the discounted nature of the ad inventory being acquired might introduce bias, encouraging agencies to recommend using certain channels to distribute advertising that they otherwise would not. Second, arbitrage adds additional unnecessary cost to advertising budgets because the agency charges a markup with no justification. These costs would be avoidable if ads were easily acquired in the programmatic marketplace.

According to one industry veteran, these practices are "happening virtually everywhere in the U.S. media landscape."[18] A major independent study commissioned by the Association of National Advertisers (ANA) in 2016 concluded that "non-transparent business practices were found to be pervasive." It went on to observe that "these practices appeared to be part of the regular course of business" across a cross section of major agencies and agency holding companies interviewed for the report.[19] One former executive stated that the entire system of agencies and clients was "one massive arbitrage system."[20]

Agencies remain a significant part of the digital advertising ecosystem and play a major role in coordinating advertising campaigns and spending. The prevalence of arbitrage means that these agencies have a strong incentive to aggressively inflate the value of the inventory they are selling. This inflates the market bubble even as the value of this ad inventory declines. Like the ratings agencies in the march to the subprime mortgage crisis, marketing agencies have conflicted incentives to give figurative AAA ratings to low-value ad inventory, because they profit directly from doing so.

This may explain why, despite growing concern from advertisers and its negative impact on major agencies, the arbitrage conflict has not been addressed in a serious way.

In 2018, two years after the ANA report, the industry publication *Digiday* opined that "advertisers and agencies talk about transparency a lot but often look as though they'd rather blame one another for the lack of clarity than come up with a way to get it." It quoted a representative of the ANA who noted that "trust between advertisers and agencies is lower than it's ever been because agencies keep denying that there are transparency issues [around arbitrage]."[21]

Ad Technology

The opacity introduced by the speed and scale of programmatic exchanges doesn't just make it more difficult to know where ads will end up online. It also makes it hard to determine why a particular unit of ad inventory commands the price that it does. Ad technology platforms, we will see, inflate prices in very much the same way that marketing agencies do.

As we discussed earlier, the programmatic marketplace relies on the interaction between two types of platforms. On the one hand, there are the demand-side platforms (DSPs), which help advertisers purchase ad inventory. On the other, there are the supply-side platforms (SSPs), which contract with publishers and obtain the privilege of offering their ad inventory to buyers.

These platforms are not neutral players in the marketplace. DSPs and SSPs have been known to work together to inflate ad prices in order to secure profit for themselves. Controversially, these practices are not typically disclosed to the advertisers and publishers whose interests the platforms ostensibly serve.

DSPs can sign bulk purchase deals to acquire inventory from their supply-side counterparts at a discounted price. This discounted inventory is then sold by the DSP at a huge markup with no disclosure of the increased cost. These margins, which are occasionally disclosed in the public Securities and Exchange Commission (SEC) filings of some DSPs, can range from 44 percent to 66 percent.[22]

SSPs, for their part, have in a number of cases misrepresented the relationships they have with various publishers and the types of inventory they are authorized to sell on their behalf. When a buyer goes to purchase this inventory, the platform simply resells inventory purchased from other SSPs.[23] In these cases, the SSP is an unnecessary middleman, artificially inflating the price paid by the ultimate buyer.

Imagine that you're a car company, looking to place an ad promoting your newest model. Using your DSP, you—or more likely an algorithm working on your behalf—identify a perfect opportunity to place an ad on *Car Central*, a prominent blog for automobile enthusiasts. As far as you know, the system works great: you bid on the spot, you win the auction, and your ad goes up on the website.

But sometimes, the DSP and the SSP are actually working against you. The DSP obtained the *Car Central* inventory at a much lower price and sold it to you at a significant, undisclosed markup. The SSP offering the *Car Central* placement might not even have access to *Car Central*—they bought the ad inventory from an SSP with access and then offered it at a significant, undisclosed markup.

In either case, you pay far more for your *Car Central* ad than you should. The cumulative effect of these undisclosed margins on price is massive. One study by *The Guardian* suggests that some 70 percent of the money spent by buyers is consumed by the ad tech platform, with the publisher retaining the remainder.[24] Had you been able to negotiate directly with *Car Central* or with an authorized SSP selling inventory on its behalf, you might have been able to avoid the hidden fees.

This arrangement creates a significant price mismatch between what a buyer pays for an ad placement and what the publisher selling that ad placement actually receives. Some publishers have responded with legal action. In 2017, *The Guardian* sued Rubicon Project, an advertising exchange, for charging additional fees to buyers of *Guardian* inventory without disclosing them to the publisher.[25] Though the case settled without any admission of liability, Rubicon Project has since eased up on the hidden fees.

Like the financial institutions that originated, packaged, and sold mortgage-backed securities in the 2000s, the operators of the programmatic advertising infrastructure have perverse incentives to keep prices high and the market hot. The introduction of hidden fees helps to artificially inflate the price of advertising inventory, even as the quality of attention captured by that advertising declines.

The overall impact of these shenanigans is twofold. First and most obviously, prices will remain inflated, imposing costs on advertisers and publishers. Less obvious but more dangerous in the long run is that these profits eliminate any incentives to change practices within the industry. The money is simply too good. It will keep the market from adjusting quickly and appropriately to structural weaknesses in the value of online advertising, allowing the formation of a bubble that will continue to grow until it pops.

What Comes Next?

Market bubbles are the result of harmful, self-reinforcing cycles between buyers and sellers that escalate out of control. These cycles can be surprisingly robust, and bubbles can continue growing long after the underlying economic situation has changed. Mortgage-backed securities continued to inflate home values long after a close look at mortgages would have revealed the inability of a massive number of borrowers to repay the loans.

The same is true in the online advertising space. Digital marketing is succeeding in spite of the deep structural issues of fraud, opacity, and falling effectiveness. The shrinking of legacy advertising channels has produced a stream of dollars largely unresponsive to these problems. At the same time, agencies and ad technology companies face perverse incentives to avoid slowing this flow of dollars and, quite the opposite, work to constantly juice the marketplace. The result is that the market for digital advertising grows, divorced from the reality of how ads are actually functioning.

Bubbles pop, of course. And when they do, it's loud.

6

Exploding the Bubble

Commodifying attention has had a huge impact on the development of the internet. On the one hand, it has enabled massive economic growth and made a wide set of online services accessible to the public in a way that they might not otherwise have been. On the other hand, commodification has introduced a range of structural vulnerabilities that raise questions about the long-term sustainability of the modern model of digital advertising, and therefore the internet itself.

The previous few chapters have laid out this case, outlining how the confluence of opacity, falling asset values, and bad incentives seem to echo previous crises. The financial crisis of 2008 has served as an uncannily good guide in highlighting the corrosive market dynamics playing out in today's online attention markets.

So what should be done about the precarious state of this economy? Advertising has been the dominant model for making money on the internet in the last few decades. But if the market is fundamentally unstable over the long term, as the financial markets were before the subprime mortgage crisis, what should we do about it?

We should see these structural instabilities as an opportunity. Online advertising has long exerted a corrosive effect on the design of the internet, and the perverse incentives to inflate the bubble make it difficult for alternative business models to emerge. Rather than trying to fix a broken market, we should work toward a controlled demolition that reduces its influence in the long run. The vulnerabilities I have laid out chart a path forward, not toward fixing what has long been a problematic system, but toward starting the internet anew.

Against Programmatic Advertising

There are good reasons to dislike the online advertising economy. Many of these critiques are well established and have existed since advertising emerged as the primary business model for funding the internet.

First, an advertising-driven online economy relies on effectively invading the privacy of consumers, a model that critics have labeled "surveillance capitalism."[1] Second, incentives exist for online platforms to continuously manipulate user behavior and seize user attention in ways that may be harmful to mental health and personal development.[2] Third, online advertising incentives promote the creation of media that is shocking or reaffirming to the viewer, producing polarization and supporting the formation of echo chambers.[3] These long-standing critiques have been an aspect of commentary about the internet for decades. One early web pioneer involved in the creation of the pop-up ad, Ethan Zuckerman, has called advertising the internet's "original sin."[4]

These are general arguments against online advertising. The rise of programmatic advertising—as a distinctly commodified, financialized means of buying and selling attention online—adds a unique set of ills to this list.

Commodification implies standardization. In online advertising, buyers want to know exactly how much attention they can purchase with their available budget. Publishers want to streamline sales by providing a simple menu of attention inventory to buy. This requires that online platforms be actively architected in a way that standardizes user engagement and attention.

In *Seeing Like a State*, James C. Scott explores a helpful notion of what he terms "legibility." In order to administrate at scale, governments and large bureaucracies need to be able to see the world effectively. The result is that the world is actively shaped in order to enable administration. To set up a system of taxation, for instance, it is necessary to create a system of fixed identities so that the government can track over time which people have paid their taxes. Establishing a legible system of fixed identities may necessitate cultural changes, like introducing the concept of a last name to cultures that previously did not have one.[5]

Legibility has shaped the media channels through which advertising has flowed. The creation of the television sitcom, with its consistent, recognizable setting and characters, is historically linked to advertising sponsors' need to approve content and promote products.[6]

Social media is no different. The need to create a liquid market in human attention influences the architecture of the social spaces of the web. Commodification requires attention to be legible: in other words, the internet must structure "engagement" in a way that is easy and accurate to measure.

Social interaction between people is mediated by structured tags such as "like" and "favorite" because these render sentiment easy to measure. Even features that we take for granted, such as requiring user registration to create a profile, are building blocks designed to support the delivery of advertising online.[7]

We've lived for so long in an online social universe purpose-built for advertising that it is difficult to imagine what an alternative might look like. Consider for a moment an alternative social media platform that we'll call Super Social Media 3000 (SSM 3000), the bizarro opposite of the advertising-legible sites we use every day. It consists of a single page on which everyone interacts and where everyone sees the same thing. Rather than having structured text boxes, users manually draw shapes and words with their cursors. There are no user profiles, and you do not need to be logged in to use it.

This is an advertising nightmare! The contributions of users are all jumbled up into an unrecognizable mess. The system logs no demographic information relevant for delivering advertising. In contrast to the discrete, measurable likes on a post on Facebook, a given section of SSM 3000 provides advertisers with only a difficult-to-interpret doodle.

SSM 3000 would assuredly be a social experience. Users would interact with one another, and would likely make friends and even build communities. But light-years of difference would exist between it and what we currently understand as "social media." The difference is a distinct lack of the features that advertising has incentivized and helped mold. By and large, we don't have platforms like SSM 3000. This is because the broad range of expression that the internet might otherwise enable has been limited to ways of connecting that are consistent with the financial needs of advertising. The free-form scribblings of SSM 3000 are financially un-sustainable compared to the shallow paradigm of likes, retweets, and short comments. In this sense, advertising is complicit in restricting the grammar of social interaction online.

Even worse, commodification is similar to other pro-cesses of standardization in that it forces new entrants to comply with the existing state of play in the market. The next Facebook or Google, to the extent that it is also driven by advertising, will need to structure attention in a way that makes its attention inventory salable in the broader marketplace. This means that securitization may be a one-way street: decisions made in the formative stage of the web limit what is possible in the future.

This is more than simply enforcing a certain kind of product design. We have been taught to interact with other people online by platforms built to buy and sell attention. One wonders if that will constrain the social possibilities of the future. At first glance, it might seem that no one would want to use SSM 3000: the anonymity and lack of clear individual spaces might degrade into a digital wall of bathroom graffiti in a few hours (or less). I don't doubt that it would.

But that deterioration says less about fundamental human nature than it says about how we have *learned* to interact online. Society has only constructed online communities within the context of a web structured by online advertising, and so no norms and practices currently exist for using a space like SSM 3000. In this sense, we may be locked in. Our ingrained approach to interacting with others online assumes the features of an advertising-driven internet. This may make it hard or impossible to build alternative online social networks that do not collapse into anarchy.

These numerous arguments amount to a condemnation of the financialized infrastructure that enables much of the web to function. There is, if anything, a strong ethical imperative to allow the collapse of global surveillance capitalism rather than attempting to save it, because it might clear the deck for something better to emerge.

Controlled Demolition

The companies built on digital advertising are an imposing part of the economic landscape. Google and Facebook appear to occupy an impregnable position, sucking in an ever-increasing amount of cash with no end in sight. Throughout the web, programmatic advertising remains pervasive, a dominant paradigm for making platforms financially sustainable if not extraordinarily profitable.

This makes discussions of how to structurally alter the web feel futile. It seems impossible to tear out the money machine powering the internet, and of little use to create alternatives when the existing model is so ingrained and so profitable. Programmatic advertising simply seems like the state of affairs that will govern the structure of the internet forever. The problems that come with these monetization models, too, appear to be chronic, always mitigated but never truly resolved.

Against this backdrop, the structural issues at the heart of programmatic advertising present not a threat but an opportunity. The collapse of the global digital advertising markets would produce a great opportunity for alternative business models to take shape, and a chance for the internet itself to take a different shape as well.

We could take an approach of benign neglect here. If one buys the argument that ad fraud, ad blocking, and an ever-increasing indifference toward ads will eventually break this marketplace on their own, why not just sit back and let it self-destruct?

Patiently waiting for programmatic advertising to break is an attractive position because it demands little of us, but it misses the bigger picture for a number of reasons. First, bubbles grow larger over time. The bigger the bubble, the harder the fall. From an economic management perspective, it is far better for a bubble to collapse early than for it to grow to a size where a market panic could produce massive collateral damage throughout the economy. As we have seen, the industry is well aware of the structural issues that threaten to upend the viability of the programmatic advertising markets, but is unlikely to make the radical changes necessary to address these problems. This will lead to partial, temporary fixes that only prolong the growth of the bubble and the associated problems that come with it.

Second, waiting for the bubble to burst on its own deprives us of the ability to distribute the social costs of such a downturn in a just and equitable manner. It is important to remember that it is not just huge advertisers and dominant digital platforms that rely on the continued functioning of the online advertising ecosystem. Like it or not, advertising is a critical, if tenuous, force for funding journalists and a vast universe of smaller media outlets and niche media.[8] They too would feel the costs of a widespread failure in the online advertising markets.

These linkages go beyond the media. One of the perverse developments of online advertising is that its outsize profitability has allowed it to float enterprises that might otherwise be insolvent. Like the banks during the subprime crisis, dense links between advertising-driven businesses and the rest of the economy mean that vulnerability in the attention marketplace may produce harm in other, less expected places. The sudden collapse of the profitability of online advertising in, say, Google Search might affect the availability of free services like Google Scholar or reduce overall investment in self-driving vehicle technology.

This is not to mention the impact on society at large. In a distressed situation where previously free services throw up paywalls and limit features to premium tiers of service, accessibility will turn on the ability to pay. Not everyone will be able to afford a subscriber-only version of the web, and such a transition could deny vulnerable segments of the population access to the critical services that they have come to rely on. Failing to address these issues in advance would be a cruel kind of irresponsibility.

Third, an uncontrolled popping of the bubble is less likely to lead to permanent change. In the absence of a clearly articulated, workable alternative, one might imagine a serious downturn after which the existing advertising ecosystem dusts itself off and resumes along the same path again. That would mean the return of the same markets with the same faults. Ensuring robust, sustained change in the structure of the web requires creating the space and opportunity for real alternatives to programmatic advertising to emerge.

Like in the demolition of a building, the safest approach might be to bring about a well-considered and structured implosion, rather than allow for an out-of-control collapse that might harm bystanders and create unintentional damage elsewhere. To that end, we may not want to simply wait for the crisis to arrive. Instead, it may be important for us to actually accelerate and bring about the collapse of the programmatic advertising bubble in ways that allow us to control the consequences.

Starting a Manageable Crisis

Programmatic advertising is a bubble. The potent combination of opacity, perverse incentives, and ever-eroding value has produced this bubble. But ultimately, financial crises depend on a crisis of confidence: a spreading panic that a highly sought-after asset is perhaps worth far less than originally speculated. How might we provoke such a crisis of confidence in the online advertising economy, particularly when billions of dollars are steadfastly committed to ignoring these warning signs? Can we control that crisis in such a way that its consequences do not spin beyond our control?

We're aided by one significant difference between the mortgage-backed securities market of 2007–2008 and the programmatic advertising market of today. In the subprime crisis, the mortgages at the root of a complex system failed. Loans were issued to home buyers who were unable to pay, resulting in defaults that upended the global economy. The panic over the viability of the assets being traded in the market was, in other words, built into the very structure of these marketplaces. Once this trip wire was triggered, the resulting cascade was impossible to manage.

In contrast, the troubles that plague the advertising economy are creeping threats. People pay less and less attention to advertisements online and steadily adopt ad blocking. Click fraud has proven to be pernicious, eroding the value of advertising inventory and resisting attempts to curtail it. Trust continues to decline between ad buyers and the wide array of players in the ecosystem with conflicting goals: the agencies, ad exchanges, online platforms, and publishers that facilitate the distribution of ads online. This slow, multifaceted creep of a range of structural problems means that the market can be stepped down in stages over time, with a series of targeted crises helping to slow and eventually reverse the flow of money into the ecosystem.

Such a calibrated takedown may be more plausible than it initially appears. The erosion in trust necessary to trigger changes in the behavior of a marketplace may be smaller than you imagine. The stock market can enter a recession without every company in an economy experiencing a downturn. The subprime mortgage crisis didn't necessarily depend on every mortgage defaulting or every mortgage being subprime. Similarly, the online advertising economy can head toward a crisis without causing the collapse of advertising as a whole. The decision of a few key players to cast their lot outside the modern programmatic ecosystem could very well be sufficient to bring the various looming problems we've discussed to the fore as it has in previous market bubbles.[9]

So how do we burst this bubble? Two pillars of faith give programmatic advertising an aura of invulnerability: measurability and effectiveness. The core proposition of programmatic advertising is that it gives advertisers an unprecedented depth of accurate data about consumers, which is able to produce uniquely effective outcomes for advertisers. For supporters, this makes programmatic advertising superior to earlier, established channels for running ads like television and print. For critics, this makes programmatic advertising a particularly powerful and pernicious force in society.

Reducing confidence in the measurability and effectiveness of programmatic advertising will chip away at the willingness of ad buyers to pour money into the ecosystem. This provides a brake that we can tap in order to slow the flow of cash into the marketplace. If it turns out that the data collected by advertisers are not in fact accurate, or that the data are not in the end all that useful for shaping perceptions and behavior, then programmatic advertising is not "better" in any real sense.

Independent research may be a particularly powerful tool for shaping industry views of online advertising. One of the reasons the programmatic advertising market is so overheated is that self-interested boosters dominate the ecosystem of information. Entities like the Interactive Advertising Bureau and the Association of National Advertisers are major outlets for research on the state of the marketplace, but they simultaneously serve as advocacy organizations on behalf of the industry. The space lacks a robust, independent institution to act as a counterweight, to objectively investigate industry claims and conduct ongoing experimentation to test the health of the marketplace.

The field of economics offers an interesting template. Founded in 1920, the National Bureau of Economic Research (NBER) is a "private, non-profit, non-partisan organization dedicated to conducting economic research and to disseminating research findings among academics, public policy makers, and business professionals."[10] The NBER's first effort was a pioneering study measuring national income, a critical basic metric for measuring a "nation's economic well-being [in] quantitative form," which had previously been unknown.[11] Over the subsequent decades, the data and research released by the NBER have played a major role in shaping thinking around the economy and its management.

Imagine an NBER for the advertising space; we'll call it the National Bureau of Advertising Research (NBAR). The NBAR could conduct rigorous research on different aspects of the machinery of programmatic advertising, shedding light on previously opaque and murky elements and putting policy around the marketplace on firmer footing. This would allow elements of the bubble to be targeted selectively and focused on, tapping the brakes here and swinging a wrecking ball there as needed to reshape the size and structure of the marketplace.

Advertisers may prove to be allies and supporters of the NBAR, because they bear some of the biggest costs in the current attention marketplace. As the researcher Michael Kaplan notes, the pressure to compete for audience attention online and the declining value of programmatic ads means that the platforms "extract large price surpluses, effectively exploiting their customers [the advertisers]."[12] The NBAR would provide those customers with a way of challenging the platforms and a basis on which to exit the market.

What would the NBAR investigate first? Nico Neumann's claims—that the granular metrics and high accountability of programmatic advertising may not make any difference—might be a good place to start. Along those lines, the NBAR could investigate the intriguing anecdotal evidence that spending significantly less on online advertising actually improves outcomes for the advertiser. In 2017, Procter & Gamble slashed around $200 million of its advertising spending in the digital space, citing concerns about bot fraud and brand safety. This money was reinvested in more traditional advertising channels like television and radio. The outcome? P&G reduced its overall spending and still increased the reach of its messaging by 10 percent.[13] More concrete exploration on this front might pressure the market to price the value of online advertising accordingly.

Similar patterns have appeared among sellers of online advertising as well. In response to the new General Data Protection Regulation privacy rules in Europe, *The New York Times* shut off all open-exchange programmatic buying on its European pages in 2018, preventing ad buyers from using the rich data available about specific consumers. In theory, this should have produced a decline in the demand for the *Times*' ad inventory; ad buyers would flow to places with more user data to sell. But the paper's digital advertising revenue was not affected at all. The *Times* "briefly tested reintroducing open-exchange programmatic ad buying . . . but didn't pursue it."[14] This phenomenon has been analyzed by Dr. Alessandro Acquisti at Carnegie Mellon University, who concludes from his work that it is unclear that data-driven targeted advertising actually produces significant returns. Acquisti's team found that although targeted advertising increased revenues for publishers, it did so at the barely noticeable rate of about "$0.000008 per advertisement."[15]

Well-grounded, hard-hitting research is powerful: it will help to persuade advertisers and publishers to leave the programmatic marketplace, and may even shape the behavior of consumers at large—say, through accelerating the adoption of ad-blocking technologies or encouraging people to switch to alternative platforms not based on advertising. All this would help produce a managed crisis in subprime attention.

But we cannot be confident that the NBAR alone would bring down the programmatic marketplace, given how profitable a willful ignorance about programmatic advertising can be. The effort to help ground public and policy-maker understanding of the internet's attention marketplaces can and must be complemented by more aggressive action from activists and whistleblowers. This could take the form of a more aggressive style of research, demonstrating the vulnerabilities of the marketplace with direct action: distributing scads of faulty consumer data in order to evaluate the lack of quality control among those buying and selling these assets, or running coordinated algorithmic bidding scripts to identify how the programmatic auction system can be manipulated. Leaks can reveal the extent to which platforms, agencies, and other actors in the ecosystem are behaving badly, and simultaneously keep those actors on their toes. Anonymous online submission systems for whistleblowers to securely leak documents around wrongdoing in the digital advertising industry could be a good way to encourage this activity. These more provocative actions could help to adversarially target and demonstrate the vulnerabilities of more intransigent actors that would otherwise resist their profits shrinking.

As in the financial markets, governments and regulations will have an important role to play. The success of even a relatively tame version of the NBAR would depend on the ability of that organization to accurately assess the state of the marketplace and to conduct experiments that truly scrutinize the claims of the industry. Vested interests within these marketplaces are not likely to grant such access willingly. In the past, access to the inner workings of the programmatic advertising infrastructure has been only grudgingly given by companies after the industry has come under public criticism and business pressure. More consistent disclosure will be critical to the project of a graduated dismantling of the subprime attention bubble.

Disclosure and Stability

The toxic blend of eroding value, market opacity, and bad incentives is producing an unsustainable market due for a painful correction. Self-regulation is failing to resolve these problems in a meaningful way and bad incentives will hinder serious efforts to clean these marketplaces up. Moreover, the intertwining of the online advertising marketplace with the fate of the broader economy means that the public has a stake in the stability and operation of the business of buying and selling attention. These facts suggest an evolving role for the government in shaping the rules of play around programmatic advertising. But what form should this take?

The similarities between the financial markets and the attention markets motivate much of this book. The history of the financial markets provides a number of useful parallels to understanding the evolution of online advertising and suggests how ostensibly limitless engines of profit can be in reality quite unstable. But the long history of thinking about financial markets and their management also gives us another important thing: a grounded sense of how regulation can help to mitigate excesses in precisely the types of markets that online advertising now resembles.

While the subprime mortgage crisis has been our primary touchstone for the last few chapters, 1929 might serve as a more apt analogy than 2008 in thinking through the question of what regulation should look like. The year 1929 was the year of the Great Crash, a catastrophic collapse in the value of stocks and other securities traded on the New York Stock Exchange. Among economists, the Great Crash is historically significant because it marks the beginning of the Great Depression, which lasted for the next twelve years and represented a colossal 15 percent decline in global GDP.[16]

These events prompted the U.S. Senate Committee on Banking and Currency to investigate the crash of the New

York Stock Exchange. Later known as the Pecora Commission after its chief counsel, Ferdinand Pecora, the investigation revealed a broad array of fraudulent activities taking place within the financial sector in the years leading up to the crisis. The Pecora Commission's findings provoked a raft of new regulations during the opening days of the Roosevelt administration that fundamentally changed the operation of the financial markets in the United States.

The less-than-savory activities uncovered by the Pecora Commission will sound oddly familiar to observers of the programmatic advertising markets. Pecora found that investment banks willingly sold gigantic lots of securities on behalf of businesses and governments known to be on shaky financial footing.[17] He also investigated the use of so-called preferred lists, which provided gifts of steeply discounted securities to a circle of influential individuals who could lend aid to the banks.[18] Moreover, Pecora highlighted the role that flimsy state-level regulations played in enabling a murky environment that made it impossible for buyers of securities to assess precisely what they were purchasing.[19] It was, in short, the same set of elements present in programmatic advertising: a potent blend of market opacity, toxic assets, and conflicted players that inflated an enormous bubble in securities, which eventually burst to catastrophic effect.

The financial giants investigated by Pecora were the technology giants of their era, in terms of both their economic importance and their cultural prestige. Investment banks investigated by the commission, like J. P. Morgan

& Co., were businesses with small numbers of employees
that generated huge wealth. *Time* magazine described the
banks as "the greatest and most legendary private business[es] of modern times."[20] Banks like J. P. Morgan's—
"the most famous and powerful in the whole world"—were
condemned by the press as "fail[ing] under a test of [their]
pride and prestige."[21] To the anger of the public, Pecora
also exposed the tendency of these businesses to pay little
or no tax, a controversy echoed in modern-day investigations into the global online advertising platforms.[22]

Importantly, the Pecora Commission shone light
on the critical role that a lack of transparency played
in bringing about the Great Crash. Buyers of securities
simply could not get a full picture of what they were
purchasing or of the conflicting interests that the sellers
might have had in the transaction. Blue-sky laws, which
mandated these disclosures, operated at the state level
and were easily circumvented.[23] Rules mandated by stock
exchanges were voluntary and similarly easy to evade.[24]

The commission inspired the passage of the Securities
Act of 1933, which tackled the transparency issue head-on.
Critically, the act established a "disclosure philosophy"
that is even today "generally regarded as the appropriate
or inevitable method of regulating corporate finance."[25] In
brief, the act set up a process by which certain significant categories of securities were to be "registered" with
the Federal Trade Commission—later the Securities and
Exchange Commission—prior to being sold. The registration process requires the issuer of a security to disclose

to the public a wide range of information about the company. This includes facts about its controlling board, financials, and other key information. Individuals who sign registration statements on behalf of the company issuing securities are held legally liable for any inaccuracies in the registration statement. The assurance that these documents were signed under this threat, in turn, is designed to support investor confidence in the viability of the assets being traded in the marketplace. This basic registration framework still governs the issuance of stocks and other securities within the United States today.

The disclosure philosophy is modest in some respects. It is designed to ensure that accurate information is available, but it does not ensure that a given security is a good investment. As Franklin Delano Roosevelt wrote in a message accompanying the introduction of the 1933 act, "The Federal Government cannot and should not take any action which might be construed as approving or guaranteeing that newly issued securities are sound . . . There is, however, an obligation upon us to insist that every issue of new securities to be sold in interstate commerce shall be accompanied by full publicity and information . . . It puts the burden of telling the whole truth on the seller."[26]

In other words, the health of a marketplace does not depend on every asset being worthwhile. The Great Crash teaches that markets do not panic simply because business is bad. Panics are instead a product of the lack of trust that buyers and sellers put on information circulating in the marketplace. Opacity allows for bad behavior on the part of conflicted players and creates uncertainty about what information is reliable. These factors permit expectations within a marketplace to float far from reality before being suddenly brought back to earth. Simply put, transparency enables market stability.

The 1933 act remains a bedrock of securities law in the United States, despite the massive transformations within the economy over the decades since it was passed. While it has by no means been immune to criticism or prevented every financial crisis, there is an overall consensus that the disclosure arrangement it sets up is an important element of a stable securities market. One scholar reviewing the empirical literature on the impact of mandatory disclosure concluded that "the effects of mandatory disclosure on stock returns, volatility and financial development are consistent with mandatory disclosure often having socially beneficial effects."[27]

Something like the disclosure philosophy may be a critical piece of the puzzle in grounding the programmatic advertising markets and deflating the bubble. The 1933 act confronted a situation in the financial markets that matches the murky, highly conflicted circumstances of the online advertising markets. The boosters of online advertising have long pushed the notion that the internet is transparent and trackable in a way that earlier generations of advertising were not. But these claims fail to tell the whole story. Online advertising has introduced new blind spots and failed to address some long-standing ones. These have allowed a range of frailties to creep into the marketplace that threaten its long-term stability.

Demonstrably, the programmatic advertising market

lacks sufficient incentives for candor. The programmatic advertising industry has remained relatively opaque about the state of the overall marketplace, despite demands from ad buyers and some embarrassing investigations. Ironically, this prevailing refusal to reveal critical data about the state of programmatic advertising to the public contributes to the risk of a catastrophic implosion. Without consistent rules governing the release of these data, buyers and sellers are left reacting to a mess of partial, easily misinterpreted information that is disclosed only when doubts already loom around the veracity of claims made about the marketplace. The likely result is overreaction and potentially cascading losses of confidence.

As in 1933, ensuring that a market reflects reality may require mandating a higher level of disclosure than the industry left to its own devices would provide. Mandated disclosure also empowers research organizations to examine the state of the marketplace and conduct experiments, giving policy makers and the public a better grasp of the economic health of the internet.

So how would the disclosure philosophy of the 1933 act apply to the world of programmatic advertising? The basics would be the same: prior to offering ad inventory for sale in the programmatic marketplace, sellers of attention would be legally required to provide to the public a standardized statement of relevant information. This statement of information would shine a spotlight on precisely the areas we have covered in the course of this book. It might include detailed metrics around brand safety, performance, proof of business relationships, disclosures of conflicts, and so on.

The disclosure mandate will need teeth: these representations can and should put the company selling ad inventory on the hook if they turn out to be inaccurate later. Legal liability is perhaps the heaviest (and slowest) deterrent, but a range of potential punishments are available to those who falsify or otherwise spread misleading information in these disclosures. One might be excluded from selling advertising inventory across certain marketplaces or be clearly marked as a seller with a bad record. These disincentives would deter attempts to obfuscate the value of advertising being bought and sold.

The global scale and the rapid speed of the programmatic advertising marketplace mean that the existing process for securities cannot be adopted wholesale. Registration in the securities context frequently requires teams of attorneys working with reviewers based at the SEC who manually examine submissions. Compliance is often expensive and time-consuming.

But adapting the disclosure approach does not mean replicating it wholesale. We should implement a regime of mandated disclosure in programmatic advertising that does not come at the expense of market dynamism. Disclosures around particular types of advertising inventory might be made available in a machine-readable fashion, allowing buying and selling algorithms to quickly evaluate the information and take actions accordingly. Instead of a single, centralized bureaucracy like the SEC acting as a gatekeeper to the advertising marketplaces of the web, we might simply mandate that these disclosures flow to a more widely spread network of trusted watchdogs that can monitor and verify claims.

As with the disclosure philosophy undergirding the Securities Act of 1933, the goal of regulation in this space cannot be to guarantee that advertising *works* or will be a success. Wanamaker's dictum about the uncertainty of advertising remains relevant today: even as we are awash in data about ads and consumers, it remains in many cases impossible to know if an ad is truly effective. Advertising also remains a diverse marketplace. Buyers demand very different things of their advertising—from increasing sales to simply "positioning" their product—and that diversity of incentives is beneficial. No one entity could guarantee that a given piece of ad inventory is "worth buying." Instead, the purpose of mandated disclosure under such a regulation would be to ensure that buyers of online advertising have access to high-quality information about what it is they are buying in the first place. The decision on whether it is worth the price will be up to them.

There is no doubt that many in the programmatic advertising ecosystem will rail against the imposition of greater legal burdens on the buying and selling of ads. Similar complaints accompanied the passage of the 1933 act. But it is past time for real legal intervention in this space. The rise of the internet has produced a deep entwining of the marketplaces of advertising with the rest of the economy. This means that the public has an interest in the fate of these markets, because their fluctuations will have major implications for the critical infrastructure of the web and the dizzyingly vast ecosystem of human activity that rests upon it. We should not wait for a new Great Crash before taking action in the global attention marketplaces of the internet.

Epilogue

The economy looked great in the years leading up to the 2008 subprime mortgage crisis. Housing prices rapidly grew in the United States and throughout Europe from 2002 to 2006, profiting homeowners and spurring construction. A World Bank report assessing prospects going into 2007 and 2008 noted that the outlook appeared "fairly bright" and characterized the global economy as a "promising environment for growth."[1]

Experts missed the warning signs. The collapse of the global economy came as a shock because economists and financial regulators had their eyes elsewhere. As the historian Adam Tooze documents, numerous reports and newspaper articles of the era worried about the problems posed by "excessive public debt, underperforming schools and a Chinese sell-off" when they should have been looking at "the basic functioning of America's economy, its banks and financial markets."[2]

Experts also felt that they had conclusively solved the problems of the past. Economists of the era expressed confidence that they had finally discovered the keys to ensuring stable economic growth and had effectively eliminated the risk of a future great recession. In 2003, the economist Robert Lucas told the American Economic Association that the "central problem of depression prevention has been solved, for all practical purposes, and has in fact been solved for many decades" by economists.[3]

That a market is doing well tells us nothing about its future prospects. Indeed, the moment when the growth of a market seems inevitable is precisely when we should be most fearful about what is driving this growth, and the structural weaknesses that might be obscured by the optimism.

Online advertising appears, by all accounts, to be continuing its rise. The COVID-19 pandemic is battering the advertising economy as this book goes to press. In spite of this, Google and Facebook appear unthreatened by any serious financial distress. If anything, the giants of programmatic advertising are poised to emerge from the crisis more dominant than ever before. Overall, advertising dollars continue to flow online at a staggering rate, which means that ever more capital is tied up in the massively automated system of programmatic buying and selling.

Experts believe that they have solved some of the most enduring challenges of their field. Programmatic advertising appears to surpass all that has come before it, offering the holy grail of marketing channels: lightning-fast speed, mind-bogglingly detailed data, and incredibly low cost. Fears around the power of "micro-targeting"—the laser-focused delivery of persuasive messaging facilitated by the internet—show that even critics of the technology industry implicitly accept the claim that these advertising systems have unsurpassed potential to manipulate opinion and change public behavior.[4]

There is no doubt that in some cases online advertising is truly effective. But the everyday reality may be quite the opposite of an all-seeing, all-knowing, all-powerful promotional engine. The reality is that vast portions of the programmatic marketplace are not so much miracle cure as snake oil. On the whole, ads capture an increasingly small portion of available attention online, and what these ads do capture is shrinking in real economic value. All the while, the market remains murky and opaque, constantly oversold by an unhealthy ecosystem of conflicted players. The result is a bubble, one that cannot grow forever.

By itself, this dysfunction in the advertising industry might be a niche problem, something that keeps a handful of advertisers and publishers up at night. But the internet we have, for better or worse, is yoked to the structure and prospects of the advertising economy. If this system of advertising is brittle, then the internet as we know it is brittle. Whether we leave these marketplaces deregulated and feral or implement systems to manage them for public benefit will define not just the future of advertising, but the future of the technologies that have shaped and continue to shape our society.

Notes

Prologue

1. "eMarketer Releases New Global Media Ad Spending Estimates," eMarketer, May 7, 2018, www.emarketer.com /content/emarketer-total-media-ad-spending-worldwide -will-rise-7-4-in-2018.
2. Ibid.
3. Nico Neumann, "How Wrong Audience Targeting and AI-Driven Campaigns Undermine Brand Growth," Programmatic I/O 2019, d3w3ioujxcalzn.cloudfront.net/item_files /183e/attachments/684322/original/howwrongaudience targetingunderminebrandgrowth_niconeuman.pdf.
4. Ibid.

Introduction

1. "Horowitz Says Lack of Business Model Hampers Internet Profits," *Communications Daily*, October 3, 1996, 1.
2. "IAB Internet Advertising Revenue Report," Nov. 2018, IAB, www.iab.com/wp-content/uploads/2018/11/IAB -WEBINAR-HY18-Internet-Ad-Revenue-Report1.pdf.
3. Tess Townsend, "Google's Share of the Search Ad Market Is Expected to Grow," *Recode*, March 14, 2017, www.recode.net /2017/3/14/14890122/google-search-ad-market-share -growth.
4. "IAB Internet Advertising Revenue Report."

5. "Google, Facebook Increase Their Grip on Digital Ad Market," eMarketer, March 14, 2017, www.emarketer.com /Article/Google-Facebook-Increase-Their-Grip-on-Digital -Ad-Market/1015417.

6. "IAB Internet Advertising Revenue Report."

7. "Data Suggests Surprising Shift: Duopoly Not All-Powerful," eMarketer, March 19, 2018, www.emarketer.com/content /google-and-facebook-s-digital-dominance-fading-as -rivals-share-grows.

8. Ibid.

9. Tim Wu, *The Attention Merchants: The Epic Scramble to Get Inside Our Heads* (New York: Alfred A. Knopf, 2016), 6.

10. Zeynep Tufekci, "YouTube, the Great Radicalizer," *New York Times*, March 10, 2018, www.nytimes.com/2018 /03/10/opinion/sunday/youtube-politics-radical.html; Zeynep Tufekci, "Facebook's Ad Scandal Isn't a 'Fail,' It's a Feature," *New York Times*, Sept. 23, 2017, www .nytimes.com/2017/09/23/opinion/sunday/facebook-ad -scandal.html.

11. See "Grand Jury Indicts Thirteen Russian Individuals and Three Russian Companies for Scheme to Interfere in the United States Political System," press release, U.S. Department of Justice, Feb. 16, 2018, www.justice.gov/opa/pr /grand-jury-indicts-thirteen-russian-individuals-and -three-russian-companies-scheme-interfere.

12. Lawrence Page and Sergey Brin, "The Anatomy of a Large-Scale Hypertextual Web Search Engine," Computer Science Department, Stanford University, infolab.stanford.edu /~backrub/google.html.

13. "eMarketer Releases New Programmatic Advertising Estimates," eMarketer, April 18, 2017, www.emarketer.com /Article/eMarketer-Releases-New-Programmatic-Advertising -Estimates/1015682.

14. Lauren Fisher, "US Programmatic Digital Display Ad Spending," eMarketer, Nov. 21, 2019, www.emarketer

.com/content/us-programmatic-digital-display-ad
-spending.

15. AppNexus, "The Digital Advertising Stats You Need for 2018," www.appnexus.com/sites/default/files/whitepapers /guide-2018stats_2.pdf.

16. Ibid.

17. Ibid.

1. The Plumbing

1. Jun Wang, Weinan Zhang, and Shuai Yuan, *Display Advertising with Real-Time Bidding (RTB) and Behavioural Targeting*, July 18, 2017, arxiv.org/abs/1610.03013.

2. See, for example, Robert D. Blackwill and Meghan L. O'Sullivan, "America's Energy Edge," *Foreign Affairs*, March– April 2014, www.foreignaffairs.com/articles/united-states /2014-02-12/americas-energy-edge. The article discusses how falling energy prices driven by shale oil will affect the geopolitical balance of power.

3. See Robert E. Hall, "The Routes into and out of the Zero Lower Bound," *Economic Policy Symposium Proceedings*, Jackson Hole, Federal Reserve Bank of Kansas City (2013), 2.

4. See, for example, Seb Joseph, "Outdoor Advertising Braced for Its Programmatic Moment," *Digiday*, Sept. 26, 2018, digiday.com/marketing/outdoor-advertising-braced -programmatic-moment.

5. See, for example, Jon Swartz, "Millions of Free E-mailers Soon May Pay Fees; Yahoo, Hotmail to Start Charging for Certain Services," *USA Today*, April 1, 2002, B1.

6. See Steven Levy, *In the Plex: How Google Thinks, Works, and Shapes Our Lives* (New York: Simon & Schuster, 2011), chap. 4.

7. Ibid.

8. See, for example, Steven Levy, "Inside Facebook's AI Machine," *Wired*, Feb. 23, 2017, www.wired.com/2017/02

/inside-facebooks-ai-machine; Gideon Lewis-Kraus, "The Great A.I. Awakening," *New York Times Magazine*, Dec. 14, 2016, www.nytimes.com/2016/12/14/magazine/the-great-ai-awakening.html.

9. Devon Maloney, "Priscilla Chan and Mark Zuckerberg's 99% Pledge Is Born with Strings Attached," *Guardian*, Dec. 2, 2015, www.theguardian.com/technology/2015/dec/02/mark-zuckerberg-and-priscilla-chans-99-pledge-is-born-with-strings-attached; Mark Zuckerberg, "A Letter to Our Daughter," Facebook, Dec. 1, 2015, www.facebook.com/notes/mark-zuckerberg/a-letter-to-our-daughter/10153375081581634?pnref=story.

10. See Elizabeth Dwoskin, "WhatsApp Founder Plans to Leave After Broad Clashes with Parent Facebook," *Washington Post*, April 30, 2018, www.washingtonpost.com/business/economy/whatsapp-founder-plans-to-leave-after-broad-clashes-with-parent-facebook/2018/04/30/49448dd2-4ca9-11e8-84a0-458a1aa9ac0a_story.html.

11. Winterberry Group, "Programmatic Everywhere? Data, Technology and the Future of Audience Engagement" (white paper, Nov. 2013), www.iab.com/wp-content/uploads/2015/07/WinterberryGroupWhitePaperProgrammaticEverywhere.pdf.

12. Sarah Sluis et al., "The Top 10 Programmatic Publishers of 2018," AdExchanger, July 31, 2018, adexchanger.com/publishers/the-top-10-programmatic-publishers-of-2018.

13. Ibid.

14. Joe Pompeo, "'Everyone's for Sale': A Generation of Digital-Media Darlings Prepares for a Frigid Winter," *Vanity Fair—Hive*, Dec. 5, 2018, www.vanityfair.com/news/2018/12/a-generation-of-digital-media-darlings-prepares-for-a-frigid-winter.

15. See, for example, Astead W. Herndon, "Elizabeth Warren Proposes Breaking Up Tech Giants Like Amazon and Facebook," *New York Times*, March 8, 2019, www.nytimes.com/2019/03/08/us/politics/elizabeth-warren-amazon.html;

Margaret Harding McGill and Daniel Lippman, "White House Drafting Executive Order to Tackle Silicon Valley's Alleged Anti-conservative Bias," *Politico*, Aug. 7, 2019, www.politico.com/story/2019/08/07/white-house-tech-censorship-1639051.

2. Market Convergence

1. See, for example, Jack Kessler, "The French Minitel: Is There Digital Life Outside of the 'US ASCII' Internet? A Challenge or Convergence?," *D-Lib Magazine*, Dec. 1995, www.dlib.org/dlib/december95/12kessler.html. The article describes the French Minitel system, a precursor to the modern-day internet.
2. Robert D. Shapiro, "This Is Not Your Father's Prodigy," *Wired*, June 1, 1993, www.wired.com/1993/06/prodigy.
3. See Matthew Crain, "Financial Markets and Online Advertising: Reevaluating the Dotcom Investment Bubble," *Information, Communication, and Society* 17, no. 3 (2014), academicworks.cuny.edu/qc_pubs/157.
4. Tim Wu, *The Attention Merchants: The Epic Scramble to Get Inside Our Heads* (New York: Alfred A. Knopf, 2016), 210.
5. Ibid., 208.
6. Steven Levy, *In the Plex: How Google Thinks, Works, and Shapes Our Lives* (New York: Simon & Schuster, 2011), chap. 2.
7. Ibid., 84.
8. Ibid., 77–78.
9. Ibid., 87.
10. Ibid., 90.
11. Ibid., 94.
12. Ibid., 83.
13. Ibid., 110.
14. Ibid., 116.
15. Ibid., 118.
16. Ibid., 117.

17. Robert A. Guth and Kevin J. Delaney, "Selling Web Advertising Space Like Pork Bellies; Exchanges That Pair Buyers, Sellers for Available Ad Slots Attract Internet Giants," *Wall Street Journal*, May 29, 2007, B1.

18. Steve Lohr, "Your Ad Here," *New York Times*, May 16, 2007, H1.

19. See, for example, Mike Nolet, "Exchange v. Network, Part I: What's the Difference?," *Mike on Ads* (blog), Aug. 16, 2007, www.mikeonads.com/2007/08/16/exchange-v-network -part-i-whats-the-difference. Nolet cofounded AppNexus, one of the major exchanges in the programmatic space.

20. Louise Story, "DoubleClick to Set Up an Exchange for Buying and Selling Digital Ads," *New York Times*, April 4, 2007, C6.

21. Louise Story and Miguel Helft, "Google Buys DoubleClick for $3.1 Billion," *New York Times*, April 14, 2007, www .nytimes.com/2007/04/14/technology/14DoubleClick .html.

22. Kevin J. Delaney, "Yahoo Will Buy the Rest of Right Media," *Wall Street Journal*, April 30, 2007, A3.

23. George Gurley, "A Wealth of Ideas," *New York Times*, March 26, 2014, www.nytimes.com/2014/03/27/fashion/Michael -Walrath-Right-Media-Founder-Wealth-of-Ideas-.html.

24. Abbey Klaassen, "The Right Media Mastermind," *Advertising Age*, May 14, 2007.

25. Benjamin F. Kuo, "Interview with Jeff Green, The Trade Desk," socalTECH, March 29, 2010, www.socaltech.com /interview_with_jeff_green_the_trade_desk/s-0027709 .html.

26. Paul Durman, "'Stock Exchange' Opens for Online Advertising," *Sunday Times* (London), Feb. 18, 2007, 3.

27. Kuo, "Interview with Jeff Green."

28. Donald MacKenzie, *An Engine, Not a Camera: How Financial Models Shape Markets* (Cambridge, Mass.: MIT Press, 2008), 12.

29. See, for example, Erik Barnouw, *A History of Broadcasting in the United States*, vol. 2, *The Golden Web, 1933 to 1953* (New York: Oxford University Press, 1968); Tom Standage, *The Victorian Internet: The Remarkable Story of the Telegraph and the Nineteenth Century's On-Line Pioneers* (New York: Bloomsbury, 2014).

30. William Cronon, *Nature's Metropolis: Chicago and the Great West* (New York: W. W. Norton, 1992), chap. 3.

31. Ibid., 106–107.

32. Ibid., 126.

33. Ibid., 114.

34. Ibid., 118.

35. Ibid., 146.

36. Ibid., 110.

37. Ibid.

38. See Emily Lambert, *The Futures: The Rise of the Speculator and the Origins of the World's Biggest Markets* (New York: Basic Books, 2012).

39. "About IAB," IAB, www.iab.com/our-story.

40. "IAB Measurement Guidelines," IAB, www.iab.com/guidelines /iab-measurement-guidelines.

41. "MRC Viewable Ad Impression Measurement Guidelines," IAB Emerging Innovations Task Force, www.iab.com/wp -content/uploads/2015/06/MRC-Viewable-Ad-Impression -Measurement-Guideline.pdf.

42. Ibid.

43. "Standards, Guidelines & Best Practices," IAB, www.iab .com/guidelines/.

44. See, for example, Michael Lewis, *Flash Boys: A Wall Street Revolt* (New York: W. W. Norton, 2015), which describes how parallel developments in the financial markets produced an explosion of trading activity.

45. Raghuram G. Rajan, "Has Financial Development Made the World Riskier?" (NBER working paper, no. 11728, Nov. 2005), www.nber.org/papers/w11728.

46. Adam Tooze, *Crashed: How a Decade of Financial Crises Changed the World* (New York: Viking, 2018), 66.

47. Rajan, "Has Financial Development Made the World Riskier?," 6.

48. See, for example, NYIAX Inc., www.nyiax.com.

49. Carmen M. Reinhart and Kenneth S. Rogoff, preface to *This Time Is Different: Eight Centuries of Financial Folly* (Princeton, N.J.: Princeton University Press, 2011), xxviii.

50. See, for example, Michael Lewis, *The Big Short: Inside the Doomsday Machine* (New York: W. W. Norton, 2011), chap. 2.

51. Reinhart and Rogoff, "Preamble: Some Initial Intuitions on Financial Fragility and the Fickle Nature of Confidence," in *This Time Is Different*.

52. Reinhart and Rogoff, *This Time Is Different*, xxxiv.

53. Cyrus Sanati, "Prince Finally Explains His Dancing Comment," *DealBook* (blog), *New York Times*, April 8, 2010, dealbook.nytimes.com/2010/04/08/prince-finally-explains-his-dancing-comment.

3. Opacity

1. George Bradt, "Wanamaker Was Wrong—the Vast Majority of Advertising Is Wasted," *Forbes*, Sept. 14, 2016, www.forbes.com/sites/georgebradt/2016/09/14/wanamaker-was-wrong-the-vast-majority-of-advertising-is-wasted.

2. Owen Gibson, "Cash from Clicking," *Guardian*, April 8, 2002, www.theguardian.com/media/2002/apr/08/mondaymediasection9.

3. Miguel Helft, "Google's Net (and Stock) Up Sharply," *New York Times*, Oct. 17, 2008, B1.

4. Randall Rothenberg, "Bye-Bye," *Wired*, Jan. 1, 1998, www.wired.com/1998/01/rothenberg. Rothenberg would later become the head of the IAB.

5. "The Ultimate Marketing Machine," *Economist*, July 6, 2006, 69.

6. See Adam Berke, Gregory Fulton, and Lauren Vaccarello, *The Retargeting Playbook: How to Turn Web-Window Shoppers into Customers* (Hoboken, N.J.: Wiley, 2014).

7. See Jennifer Langston, "For $1000, Anyone Can Purchase Online Ads to Track Your Location and App Use," *UW News*, Oct. 18, 2017, www.washington.edu/news/2017/10/18/for-1000-anyone-can-purchase-online-ads-to-track-your-location-and-app-use.

8. Financial Crisis Inquiry Commission, *The Financial Crisis Inquiry Report: Final Report of the National Commission on the Causes of the Financial and Economic Crisis in the United States* (2011), 118, fraser.stlouisfed.org/title/5034. A discussion of the role of rating agencies in the crisis and the fact that certain investors were limited to buying only securities highly rated by these organizations.

9. For a useful overview of these tools, see Dominik Kosorin, *Introduction to Programmatic Advertising* (2016).

10. See, for example, Nathaniel Popper, "The Robots Are Coming for Wall Street," *New York Times Magazine*, Feb. 25, 2016, www.nytimes.com/2016/02/28/magazine/the-robots-are-coming-for-wall-street.html.

11. David Segal, "The Great Unwatched," *New York Times*, May 4, 2014, BU1.

12. Paul P. Murphy, Kaya Yurieff, and Gianluca Mezzofiore, "Exclusive: YouTube Ran Ads from Hundreds of Brands on Extremist Channels," CNNMoney, April 20, 2018, money.cnn.com/2018/04/19/technology/youtube-ads-extreme-content-investigation/index.html.

13. See, for example, Kelsey Sutton, "Advertisers Are More Concerned Than Ever About Brand Safety, According to New Study," *Adweek*, June 7, 2018, www.adweek.com/digital/advertisers-are-more-concerned-than-ever-about-brand-safety-according-to-new-study.

14. Ross Benes, "Five Charts Explaining the State of Brand Safety," eMarketer, July 27, 2018, www.emarketer.com/content/five-charts-explaining-the-state-of-brand-safety.

15. "The State of Programmatic Media Buying: New ANA Research," Advertising Research Foundation, Jan. 5, 2018, thearf.org/category/news-you-can-use/the-state-of-programmatic-media-buying-new-ana-research.

16. Kurt Wagner, "Facebook Is Hiring Another 3,000 People to Pull Down Violent and Inappropriate Content," *Recode*, May 3, 2017, www.recode.net/2017/5/3/15531478/facebook-hiring-3000-people-violent-inappropriate-video-content-post.

17. See James Vincent, "AI Won't Relieve the Misery of Facebook's Human Moderators," *The Verge*, Feb. 27, 2019, www.theverge.com/2019/2/27/18242724/facebook-moderation-ai-artificial-intelligence-platforms.

18. Benjamin Bain, "Wall Street Dark Pools to Come out of Shadows Thanks to SEC," *Bloomberg*, July 18, 2018, www.bloomberg.com/news/articles/2018-07-18/wall-street-dark-pools-set-to-come-out-of-shadows-thanks-to-sec.

19. See Michael Lewis, *Flash Boys: A Wall Street Revolt* (New York: W. W. Norton, 2015), chap. 2, which describes the problem of front-running in greater detail.

20. See Yuyu Chen, "Brands and Agencies on the Pros and Cons of Private Marketplaces," *Digiday*, Nov. 15, 2016, digiday.com/marketing/brands-agencies-pros-cons-private-marketplaces.

21. "More than 80% of Digital Display Ads Will Be Bought Programmatically in 2018," eMarketer, April 9, 2018, www.emarketer.com/content/more-than-80-of-digital-display-ads-will-be-bought-programmatically-in-2018.

22. Ross Benes, "Ad Spending on Private Marketplaces Will Pass Open Exchanges Next Year," eMarketer, May 8, 2019, www.emarketer.com/content/ad-spending-on-private-marketplaces-will-pass-open-exchanges-next-year.

23. Ken Auletta, *Frenemies: The Epic Disruption of the Ad Business (and Everything Else)* (New York: Penguin Press, 2018), chap. 7, describes the disintermediation threat online platforms pose to agencies.

24. Issie Lapowsky, "A New Facebook Lawsuit Makes 'Pivot to Video' Even More Shortsighted," *Wired*, Oct. 17, 2018, www.wired.com/story/facebook-lawsuit-pivot-to-video -mistake.

25. Facebook, "What the Shift to Video Means for Creators," Jan. 7, 2015, www.facebook.com/facebookmedia/blog/what -the-shift-to-video-means-for-creators.

26. Pavithra Mohan, "Mark Zuckerberg: Soon, the Majority of Content We Consume Will Be Video," *Fast Company*, Feb. 22, 2016, www.fastcompany.com/3057024/mark-zuckerberg -soon-the-majority-of-content-we-consume-will-be-video.

27. Heidi N. Moore, "The Secret Cost of Pivoting to Video," *Columbia Journalism Review*, Sept. 26, 2017, www.cjr.org /business_of_news/pivot-to-video.php.

28. Ibid.

29. Steven Perlberg, "Facebook Apologizes for Video Metric Miscalculation," *Wall Street Journal*, Sept. 23, 2016, www .wsj.com/articles/facebook-apologizes-for-video-metric -miscalculation-1474641054.

30. Facebook, "An Update on Metrics and Reporting," Nov. 16, 2016, www.facebook.com/business/news/metrics -reporting-update.

31. Jason Kint (@jason_kint), "Oomph. Pivotal analyst just dropped report showing Facebook Ad Manager claims 25 million more 18–34 year olds than the US census," Twitter, Sept. 5, 2017, 6:12 p.m., twitter.com/jason_kint/status /905237289588199425.

32. Sara Fischer, "Facebook Touts Video Metrics, Outlines More Scrutiny for Show Funding," *Axios*, Dec. 13, 2018, www.axios.com/facebook-touts-video-watch-platform -metrics-17385ab1-2861-4e12-a9ca-1866e1faddd8.html.

33. Kelsey Sutton, "Facebook Hid Inflated Video Ad Metrics Error for Over a Year, Advertisers Allege," *Adweek,* October 17, 2018, www.adweek.com/digital/facebook-hid-inflated -video-ad-metrics-error-for-over-a-year-advertisers-allege.

34. Ibid.

35. See Marty Swant, "Media Rating Council Gives Facebook Accreditation for Ad Impressions," *Adweek*, April 5, 2018, www.adweek.com/digital/media-rating-councils-gives -facebook-accreditation-for-ad-impressions; Babak Pahlavan, "New MRC Accreditations and Partners for Google and YouTube Ads Measurement," *Google Ads Blog*, Sept. 26, 2018, www.blog.google/products/ads/transparency-choice -ads-measurement.

36. See, for example, Pahlavan, "New MRC Accreditations and Partners for Google and YouTube Ads Measurement."

37. Allison Schiff, "Facebook and GroupM Tussle on Third-Party Viewability Verification," AdExchanger, June 3, 2015, adexchanger.com/online-advertising/facebook-and -groupm-tussle-on-third-party-viewability-verification.

4. Subprime Attention

1. Alyson Shontell, "This Playground Is a Significant Part of Twitter's Founding Story," *Business Insider*, Sept. 18, 2013, www.businessinsider.com/twitters-founding-story-south -park-san-francisco-2013-9.

2. See, generally, Gary Wolf, *Wired: A Romance* (New York: Random House, 2003), chap. 7.

3. Adrienne LaFrance, "The First-Ever Banner Ad on the Web," *Atlantic*, April 21, 2017, www.theatlantic.com/technology /archive/2017/04/the-first-ever-banner-ad-on-the-web /523728.

4. Mark Irvine, "Google Ads Benchmarks for YOUR Industry [Updated!]," *The WordStream Blog*, Aug. 27, 2019, www .wordstream.com/blog/ws/2016/02/29/google-adwords -industry-benchmarks.

5. "Social Advertising Benchmark Report," Salesforce.com, www.salesforce.com/form/marketingcloud/social-ads -benchmark.jsp. The year 2013 shows a range between 0.18 percent and 0.36 percent.

6. Google, "Better Click Quality on Display Ads Improves the User and Advertiser Experience," *Inside AdWords* (blog), June 25, 2015, adwords.googleblog.com/2015/06/better-click-quality-on-display-ads.html.

7. "Comscore and Starcom USA Release Updated 'Natural Born Clickers' Study Showing 50 Percent Drop in Number of U.S. Internet Users Who Click on Display Ads," Comscore, Oct. 1, 2009, www.comscore.com/Insights/Press-Releases/2009/10/Comscore-and-Starcom-USA-Release-Updated-Natural-Born-Clickers-Study-Showing-50-Percent-Drop-in-Number-of-U.S.-Internet-Users-Who-Click-on-Display-Ads.

8. Tom Blake, Chris Nosko, and Steven Tadelis, "Consumer Heterogeneity and Paid Search Effectiveness: A Large Scale Field Experiment" (NBER working paper, no. 20171, May 2014), abstract, 32, www.nber.org/papers/w20171.

9. Randall A. Lewis and David H. Reiley, "Advertising Effectively Influences Older Users: How Field Experiments Can Improve Measurement and Targeting," *Review of Industrial Organization* 44, no. 2 (2014): 147–59.

10. Alex Kantrowitz, "56% of Digital Ads Served Are Never Seen, Says Google," *AdAge*, Dec. 3, 2014, adage.com/article/digital/56-digital-ads-served-google/296062.

11. "In-Target, Viewability, and Invalid Traffic: Campaign Benchmarks Across the Globe," Comscore, April 21, 2017, www.comscore.com/Insights/Blog/In-Target-Viewability-and-Invalid-Traffic-Campaign-benchmarks-across-the-globe.

12. Duncan Stewart and Mark Casey, "Are Consumers 'Adlergic'? A Look at Ad-Blocking Habits," Deloitte, deloitte.wsj.com/cmo/2018/04/03/are-consumers-adlergic-a-look-at-ad-blocking-habits.

13. "2017 Adblock Report," Blockthrough, Feb. 1, 2017, www.blockthrough.com/2017/02/01/adblockreport.

14. Ibid.

15. Ibid.

16. Michael Rosenwald, "The Digital Media Industry Needs to React to Ad Blockers . . . or Else," *Columbia Journalism Review*, Sept.–Oct. 2015, www.cjr.org/business_of_news /will_ad_blockers_kill_the_digital_media_industry .php.

17. See Facebook, Inc. Form 10-K for Fiscal Year Ended December 31, 2015, EDGAR, Securities and Exchange Commission, 2016, www.sec.gov/Archives/edgar/data/1326801 /000132680116000043/fb-12312015x10k.htm. 2015 Facebook revenue was $17.9 billion.

18. "2017 Adblock Report," Blockthrough.

19. "Ad Blocking: Who Blocks Ads, Why and How to Win Them Back," IAB, www.iab.com/wp-content/uploads /2016/07/IAB-Ad-Blocking-2016-Who-Blocks-Ads-Why -and-How-to-Win-Them-Back.pdf.

20. Randall Rothenberg, "Ad Blocking: The Unnecessary Internet Apocalypse," *AdAge*, Sept. 22, 2015, www.adage .com/article/digitalnext/ad-blocking-unnecessary -internet-apocalypse/300470.

21. Jim Leichenko, "The Most Expensive Keywords on Google—Anniversary Edition," Kantar Media, Sept. 4, 2018, www.kantar.media/eKbojrm.

22. Alexandra Bruell, "Fraudulent Web Traffic Continues to Plague Advertisers, Other Businesses," *Wall Street Journal*, March 28, 2018, www.wsj.com/articles/fraudulent-web -traffic-continues-to-plague-advertisers-other-businesses -1522234801.

23. "Ad Fraud to Cost Advertisers $19 Billion in 2018, Representing 9% of Total Digital Advertising Spend," Juniper Research, Sept. 26, 2017, www.juniperresearch.com/press /press-releases/ad-fraud-to-cost-advertisers-$19-billion-in -2018.

24. George P. Slefo, "Report: For Every $3 Spent on Digital Ads, Fraud Takes $1," *AdAge*, Oct. 22, 2015, adage.com/article /digital/ad-fraud-eating-digital-advertising-revenue/301017.

25. Susan Bidel et al., "Poor Quality Ads Cost US Marketers $7.4 Billion in 2016," Forrester Research, March 30, 2017, www.forrester.com/report/Poor+Quality+Ads+Cost+US +Marketers+74+Billion+In+2016/-/E-RES136115.

26. Ross Benes, "The State of Video Ad Fraud," *Digiday*, Nov. 2, 2017, digiday.com/marketing/state-video-ad-fraud.

27. Stuart Feil, "The Massive Scale of Mobile Ad Fraud," *Adweek*, March 22, 2018.

28. Jessica Davies, "The FT Warns Advertisers After Discovering High Levels of Domain Spoofing," *Digiday*, Sept. 27, 2017, digiday.com/media/ft-warns-advertisers-discovering -high-levels-of-domain-spoofing.

29. Michael H. Keller, "The Flourishing Business of Fake YouTube Views," *New York Times*, Aug. 11, 2018, www.nytimes .com/interactive/2018/08/11/technology/youtube-fake -view-sellers.html.

30. Craig Silverman, "Apps Installed on Millions of Android Phones Tracked User Behavior to Execute a Multimillion-Dollar Ad Fraud Scheme," *BuzzFeed News*, Oct. 23, 2018, www.buzzfeednews.com/article/craigsilverman/how -a-massive-ad-fraud-scheme-exploited-android-phones -to.

31. Lucia Moses, "'The Professionalization of Fraud': Agencies Are Alarmed by 'Methbot' Scheme," *Digiday*, Dec. 21, 2016, digiday.com/media/professionalization-fraud-agencies -alarmed-methbot-scheme.

32. Benes, "The State of Video Ad Fraud." Fraud accounts for 22 percent of ad spending in video.

33. See, generally, Ken Auletta, *Frenemies: The Epic Disruption of the Ad Business (and Everything Else)* (New York: Penguin Press, 2018), chaps. 1–2.

34. Babak Pahlavan, "New MRC Accreditations and Partners for Google and YouTube Ads Measurement," *Google Ads Blog*, Sept. 26, 2018, www.blog.google/products/ads /transparency-choice-ads-measurement; Allison Schiff, "Facebook and GroupM Tussle on Third-Party Viewability

Verification," AdExchanger, June 3, 2015, adexchanger
.com/online-advertising/facebook-and-groupm-tussle-on
-third-party-viewability-verification.

35. "Ads.Txt—Authorized Digital Sellers," IAB Tech Lab,
iabtechlab.com/ads-txt.

36. Ross Benes, "The State of Ads.Txt," *Digiday*, Jan. 22, 2018,
digiday.com/marketing/state-ads-txt.

37. Bruce Schneier, "Detecting Adblocker Blockers," *Schneier
on Security* (blog), Jan. 5, 2018, www.schneier.com/blog
/archives/2018/01/detecting_adblo.html.

38. Sapna Maheshwari, "Adblock Plus, Created to Protect
Users from Ads, Instead Opens the Door," *New York Times*,
Sept. 18, 2016, www.nytimes.com/2016/09/19/business
/media/adblock-plus-created-to-protect-users-from-ads
-opens-the-door.html.

39. Sam Barker, "Future Digital Advertising: AI, Ad Fraud,
and Ad Blocking, 2017–2022," Juniper Research, www
.juniperresearch.com/researchstore/content-commerce
/future-digital-advertising.

40. Ross Benes, "Study: Top Publishers Like *The New York
Times* and *The Washington Post* Lose $3.5 Million a Day to
Domain Spoofing," *Digiday*, Dec. 12, 2017, digiday.com
/media/using-ads-txt-publishers-catch-buyers-spending-1
-billion-year-fake-video-inventory.

41. "Ads.Txt Reduces Ad Fraud by 10%, but Double-Digit Ad
Fraud Rates Persist," *Pixalate Blog*, Sept. 25, 2018, blog
.pixalate.com/does-ads-txt-reduce-ad-fraud.

42. Ross Benes, "How Publishers Are Getting Fooled by Ads.
Txt Fraud," *Digiday*, Nov. 6, 2017, digiday.com/media
/publishers-getting-fooled-ads-txt-fraud.

43. Lara O'Reilly, "Scammers Target Ad Industry's Initiative to
Thwart Fraud," *Wall Street Journal*, Feb. 7, 2019, www.wsj
.com/articles/scammers-target-ad-industrys-initiative-to
-thwart-fraud-11549537200.

44. Patrick Kulp, "Mobile Ad Fraud Is Surging as Scammers Get
Smarter, According to New Report," *Adweek*, May 24, 2018,

www.adweek.com/digital/mobile-ad-fraud-is-surging-as
-scammers-get-smarter-researchers-say.

45. "2017 Adblock Report," Blockthrough.

46. Garett Sloane, "Snapchat May Force Users to Watch
Three Seconds of Ads Before Skipping," *AdAge*, Jan. 2,
2018, adage.com/article/digital/snapchat-considers-making
-users-sit-3-seconds-ads/311775.

47. Alison McCarthy, "Millennials and YouTube Ads: Most
Watch Until They Can Skip," eMarketer, Jan. 6, 2017,
www.emarketer.com/Article/Millennials-YouTube-Ads
-Most-Watch-Until-They-Skip/1014979.

5. Inflating the Bubble

1. Ben S. Bernanke, "The Global Saving Glut and the U.S. Current Account Deficit" (remarks at the Sandridge Lecture,
Virginia Association of Economists, Richmond, March 10,
2005), www.federalreserve.gov/boarddocs/speeches/2005
/200503102.

2. Financial Crisis Inquiry Commission, *The Financial Crisis
Inquiry Report: Final Report of the National Commission on
the Causes of the Financial and Economic Crisis in the United
States* (2011), 104, fraser.stlouisfed.org/title/5034.

3. Joint Center for Housing Studies of Harvard University,
"The State of the Nation's Housing, 2008," www.jchs
.harvard.edu/sites/default/files/son2008.pdf.

4. Martin Wolf, *The Shifts and the Shocks: What We've Learned—
and Have Still to Learn—from the Financial Crisis* (New York:
Penguin Books, 2015), chap. 5.

5. "eMarketer Releases New Global Media Ad Spending Estimates," eMarketer, May 7, 2018, www.emarketer.com
/content/emarketer-total-media-ad-spending-worldwide
-will-rise-7-4-in-2018.

6. See, for example, Robert Seamans and Feng Zhu, "Re-
sponses to Entry in Multi-sided Markets: The Impact of
Craigslist on Local Newspapers," *Management Science* 60,

no. 2 (Feb. 2014): 476–93. This article describes a 2013 study estimating a $5 billion loss to newspapers as a result of Craigslist.

7. Jasmine Enberg, "Global Digital Ad Spending 2019," eMarketer, March 28, 2019, www.emarketer.com/content/global -digital-ad-spending-2019.

8. See "US TV Ad Spending to Fall in 2018," eMarketer, March 28, 2018, www.emarketer.com/content/us-tv-ad -spending-to-fall-in-2018.

9. See Heather Connon, "Why Ninja Mortgages Could Wreak Havoc," *Observer* (London), Sept. 30, 2007, www.theguardian .com/business/2007/sep/30/5.

10. See Adam Tooze, *Crashed: How a Decade of Financial Crises Changed the World* (New York: Viking, 2018), 49, which discusses the incentives of ratings agencies to be "helpful."

11. Ibid., 70.

12. See, for example, Gretchen Morgenson and Louise Story, "Banks Bundled Bad Debt, Bet Against It and Won," *New York Times*, Dec. 23, 2009, www.nytimes.com/2009/12/24 /business/24trading.html.

13. See Michael Farmer, *Madison Avenue Manslaughter: An Inside View of Fee-Cutting Clients, Profit-Hungry Owners and Declining Ad Agencies*, 2nd ed. (New York: LID, 2017).

14. See, for example, Jeff Beer, "Why Ad Agencies Shouldn't Fear Facebook's Creative Shop," *Fast Company*, April 12, 2017, www.fastcompany.com/40405239/why-ad-agencies -shouldnt-fear-facebooks-creative-shop.

15. Seb Joseph, "Ad Quality Rises to the Top of the Agenda for Media Agency Reviews," *Digiday*, Jan. 20, 2018, digiday .com/marketing/ad-quality-rises-top-agenda-media -agency-reviews.

16. See Ken Auletta, *Frenemies: The Epic Disruption of the Ad Business (and Everything Else)* (New York: Penguin Press, 2018), chap. 1.

17. See Jessica Davies, "'Data Arbitrage Is as Big a Problem as Media Arbitrage': Confessions of a Media Exec," *Digiday*, Dec. 11, 2017, digiday.com/media/data-arbitrage-big-problem -media-arbitrage-confessions-media-exec.

18. Jack Neff, "Former Mediacom CEO Alleges Widespread U.S. Agency 'Kickbacks,'" *AdAge*, March 6, 2015, adage .com/article/agency-news/mediacom-ceo-mandel-skewers -agencies-incentives/297470.

19. "An Independent Study of Media Transparency in the U.S. Advertising Industry," K2 Intelligence, June 7, 2016, online.wsj.com/public/resources/documents/Transparency .pdf.

20. Jessica Davies, "Confessions of an Ex-brand Global Media Chief: 'It's All One Massive Arbitrage System,'" *Digiday*, May 23, 2017, digiday.com/media/confessions-ex-brand -global-media-chief-one-massive-arbitrage-system.

21. Seb Joseph, "Two Years After the ANA's Report, a Cloud Still Hangs over Media Transparency," *Digiday*, July 16, 2018, digiday.com/marketing/two-years-anas-report-cloud-still -hangs-media-transparency.

22. Ross Benes, "Ad Buyer, Beware: How DSPs Sometimes Play Fast and Loose," *Digiday*, May 25, 2017, digiday.com /marketing/dsp-squeeze-buyers.

23. Ross Benes, "'We Go Straight to the Publisher': Buyers Beware of SSPs Arbitraging Inventory," *Digiday*, Feb. 16, 2017, digiday.com/media/ssp-arbitrage.

24. David Pidgeon, "Where Did the Money Go? *Guardian* Buys Its Own Ad Inventory," Mediatel, Oct. 4, 2016, mediatel.co.uk/newsline/2016/10/04/where-did-the-money -go-guardian-buys-its-own-ad-inventory.

25. Ronan Shields, "Rubicon Project and *The Guardian* Resolve Legal Dispute over 'Hidden' Fees," *Adweek*, Oct. 12, 2018, www.adweek.com/programmatic/rubicon-project-and-the -guardian-resolve-legal-dispute-over-hidden-fees.

6. Exploding the Bubble

1. See, for example, Shoshana Zuboff, *The Age of Surveillance Capitalism: The Fight for a Human Future at the New Frontier of Power* (New York: PublicAffairs, 2019).

2. Ibid., chap. 10.

3. See, for example, Eli Pariser, *The Filter Bubble: How the New Personalized Web Is Changing What We Read and How We Think* (New York: Penguin Books, 2012).

4. Ethan Zuckerman, "The Internet's Original Sin," *Atlantic*, Aug. 14, 2014, www.theatlantic.com/technology/archive/2014/08/advertising-is-the-internets-original-sin/376041/.

5. James C. Scott, *Seeing Like a State: How Certain Schemes to Improve the Human Condition Have Failed* (New Haven, Conn.: Yale University Press, 1999).

6. Erik Barnouw, *A History of Broadcasting in the United States*, vol. 3, *The Image Empire, from 1953* (New York: Oxford University Press, 1970), 36–38.

7. See, for example, Gary Wolf, *Wired: A Romance* (New York: Random House, 2003), 107, noting that the rationale for requiring user registration was to "give sponsors exact information about viewers and eventually allow targeted advertisements to hit specific users."

8. See, for example, Matt Haughey, "State of MetaFilter," *MetaTalk*, May 19, 2014, metatalk.metafilter.com/23245/State-of-MetaFilter; Tavi Gevinson, "Editor's Letter," *Rookie*, Nov. 30, 2018, www.rookiemag.com/2018/11/editors-letter-86.

9. See Robert J. Shiller, *Irrational Exuberance* (Princeton, N.J.: Princeton University Press, 2000), chap. 7, which discusses the psychological role of "anchors" in determining market bubbles.

10. "About the NBER," National Bureau of Economic Research, www.nber.org/info.html.

11. See Solomon Fabricant, *Toward a Firmer Basis of Economy Policy: The Founding of the National Bureau of Economic*

Research (Cambridge, Mass.: National Bureau of Economic Research, 1984), 11, www.nber.org/nberhistory/sfabricantrev.pdf.

12. Michael Kaplan, "The Self-Consuming Commodity: Audiences, Users, and the Riddle of Digital Labor," *Television and New Media* 21, no. 3 (Jan. 11, 2019), 240–59.

13. Lauren Johnson, "When Procter & Gamble Cut $200 Million in Digital Ad Spend, It Increased Its Reach 10%," *Adweek*, March 1, 2018, www.adweek.com/brand-marketing/when-procter-gamble-cut-200-million-in-digital-ad-spend-its-marketing-became-10-more-effective/amp.

14. Jessica Davies, "After GDPR, *The New York Times* Cut Off Ad Exchanges in Europe—and Kept Growing Ad Revenue," *Digiday*, Jan. 16, 2019, digiday.com/media/new-york-times-gdpr-cut-off-ad-exchanges-europe-ad-revenue.

15. Natasha Lomas, "The Case Against Behavioral Advertising Is Stacking Up," *TechCrunch*, Jan. 20, 2019, social.techcrunch.com/2019/01/20/dont-be-creepy.

16. Roger Lowenstein, "Economic History Repeating," *Wall Street Journal*, Jan. 13, 2015, www.wsj.com/articles/book-review-hall-of-mirrors-by-barry-eichengreen-1421192283.

17. See Joel Seligman, *The Transformation of Wall Street: A History of the Securities and Exchange Commission and Modern Corporate Finance* (New York: Aspen, 2003), 26–28.

18. Ibid., 34–35.

19. Ibid., 44–46.

20. Ibid., 31.

21. Ibid., 37.

22. See, for example, David Pegg, "The Tech Giants Will Never Pay Their Fair Share of Taxes—Unless We Make Them," *Guardian*, Dec. 11, 2017, www.theguardian.com/commentisfree/2017/dec/11/tech-giants-taxes-apple-paradise-corporation-avoidance.

23. Seligman, *Transformation of Wall Street*, 44.

24. Ibid., 46.

25. Ibid., 39.

26. Ibid., 53.

27. Allen Ferrell, "The Case for Mandatory Disclosure in Securities Regulation Around the World" (Harvard Law and Economics Discussion Paper no. 492, Sept. 2004), www.ssrn.com/abstract=631221.

Epilogue

1. World Bank, *Global Economic Prospects 2007: Managing the Next Wave of Globalization* (Washington, D.C.: World Bank, 2006), elibrary.worldbank.org/doi/book/10.1596/978-0-8213-6727-8.

2. See Adam Tooze, *Crashed: How a Decade of Financial Crises Changed the World* (New York: Viking, 2018), 42–43.

3. Robert E. Lucas, Jr., "Macroeconomic Priorities," *American Economic Review* 93, no. 1 (2003).

4. See, for example, Dipayan Ghosh and Ben Scott, "Facebook's New Controversy Shows How Easily Online Political Ads Can Manipulate You," *Time*, March 19, 2018, time.com/5197255/facebook-cambridge-analytica-donald-trump-ads-data.

Acknowledgments

I'd like to thank Moira Weigel, Ben Tarnoff, Jackson Howard, Emily Bell, and the teams at *Logic* and FSG, who encouraged me to write this book and offered invaluable advice throughout the entire process. I'd also like to acknowledge Adi Kamdar, whose collaboration with me on a 2013 paper about "peak ads" inspired many of the arguments contained in these pages. Finally, I'd like to extend a special thanks to Lea Rosen, whose tireless editing and frank feedback over the past year have sharpened my thinking and made the book orders of magnitude better.